PUFFIN BOOKS

E. YOUNG

THE ASTRONAUT'S SURVIVAL GUIDE

PUFFIN BOOKS

Published by the Penguin Group
Penguin Books Ltd, 80 Strand, London WC2R ORL, England
Penguin Group (USA), Inc., 375 Hudson Street, New York, New York 10014, USA
Penguin Books Australia Ltd, 250 Camberwell Road, Camberwell, Victoria 3124, Australia
Penguin Books Canada Ltd, 10 Alcorn Avenue, Toronto, Ontario, Canada M4V 3B2
Penguin Books India (P) Ltd, 11 Community Centre, Panchsheel Park,
New Delhi — 110 017, India
Penguin Group (NZ), cnr Airborne and Rosedale Roads, Albany, Auckland 1310,
New Zealand
Penguin Books (South Africa) (Pty) Ltd, 24 Sturdee Avenue, Rosebank 2196, South Africa

Penguin Books Ltd, Registered Offices: 80 Strand, London WC2R ORL, England

www.penguin.com

First published 2004
1 3 5 7 9 10 8 6 4 2

Text copyright © Emma Young, 2004
Design and illustrations by John Fordham
All rights reserved

The moral right of the author has been asserted

Picture Credits
Dennis Tito (page 19) © AP/Wide World Photos.
Isaac Newton (page 23) © CORBIS.
All other pictures courtesy of NASA.

Made and printed in England by Clays Ltd, St Ives plc

British Library Cataloguing in Publication Data
A CIP catalogue record for this book is available from the British Library

ISBN 0—141—31658—6

CONTENTS

One hundred kilometres from your front door is another world.

It's freezing cold and boiling hot.

It's packed with deadly shrapnel and killer rays.

It's the most beautiful, the most dangerous, the most exciting place ...

... It's space!

If you are dreaming of blasting off from Earth, you have two options:

1. Carry on dreaming.

2. Get real – and achieve that dream.

Whether you want to join the elite corps of highly trained astronauts, or hand over giant wads of cash to pay for a ticket on a spaceship, you'll need to be prepared.

You'll need advice.

You'll need a guide.

You'll need this book.

*I'm going to be your guide. My name is **Bill Brain**, ZVV News's top space correspondent, and this, candidate astronaut, is your passport to space.*

THE RIGHT STUFF

What do a Russian dog, a pizza and a golf ball have in common?
Answer: They've all been into space!

Want to follow them?

First, you'll need to decide who you want to fly with. Only three countries have ever blasted people into orbit: Russia, the USA and China.

To fly on a Chinese spacecraft, you'll have to be from China. But both Russia and the USA send up space travellers from all over the world.

If you fly with the Americans, you'll be an astronaut (the word comes from the Greek for star sailor). If you go with the Russians, you'll be a cosmonaut (universe sailor). Same job, different name.

Then you'll need to pass the strict selection tests. These tests will make you vomit. They'll probe your mind. They'll push you to your limits. They could have you screaming to stay on Earth for the rest of your life!

But wait. What could be easier than floating around in space? Anyone could do it, even your grandma. Right?

Well, if she's the type of grandma who prefers a 10-kilometre jog before breakfast to baking cakes, she might. After all, a 77-year-old recently visited the International Space Station.

BILL BRAIN'S HALL OF ASTRO FAME   no. 1

John Herschel Glenn Jr
- *The first American to orbit Earth*
- *The oldest astronaut in space*

Born: 1921, USA

In 1962, John Glenn became the first American to orbit Earth. He retired from NASA in 1965, later becoming elected a US senator. In 1998, aged 77, Glenn became the oldest person ever to go into space. He served on a nine-day mission, partly to investigate space and the ageing process.

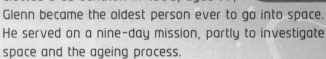

Despite his age, John Glenn was very healthy and active. And even he had to pass tough physical exams.

How tough those exams are depends on what type of star sailor you want to be ...

Have you got the right stuff?

The National Aeronautics and Space Administration (NASA) in the USA has the job of choosing who can become an astronaut. About every two years NASA selects around 20 lucky and very hard-working men and women to become:

Pilots

Every space mission has two pilot astronauts, one of whom is also the 'mission commander'. He or she is in charge of the crew and the safety and success of the mission.

EXPERIENCE NEEDED:
· At least 1,000 hours' flying time in a jet plane.
· A degree in science or maths, plus a further degree or three years' experience as a scientist.

BASIC REQUIREMENTS:
· 20/70 vision. This is good vision, which can be corrected to perfect vision with glasses or contact lenses. Next time you visit the optician, ask them if you have 20/70 or better.
· Height between 1.63 and 1.93 metres.
· Must be an American citizen.

Mission specialists

The mission specialist helps with general operations, performs space walks and conducts experiments.

EXPERIENCE NEEDED:
· A degree in maths or science plus a further degree, or three years' experience as a scientist.

BASIC REQUIREMENTS:
· 20/200 vision. This isn't as good as the vision you'll need to be a pilot – but it must be correctable to perfect.
· Height between 1.49 and 1.93 metres.

But not all mission specialists are American citizens. They can also be ...

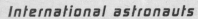 International astronauts

NASA has an agreement with Canada, Japan, Russia, Brazil and Europe to train astronauts selected by their space agencies. The astronauts then serve as mission specialists. (The Russian Aviation and Space Agency, properly called Rosaviakosmos, has a similar agreement with the USA and other countries, including India and China.)

There is one other astronaut type:

Payload specialists

These astronauts have special skills needed for a mission. They might be working as engineers or scientists for private companies, expert in whatever cargo is flying on a shuttle. John Glenn flew as a payload specialist in 1998.

The basic requirements for international astronauts and payload specialists are the same as for NASA mission specialists.

Testing, testing ...

If you pass the basic physical requirements, you'll go through to the second round of medical testing. These tests are designed to check your brain, your blood, your vision and hearing, your muscles and your heart.

Blood pressure

Blood pressure is a measure of how well your heart and arteries push blood around your body. If your blood pressure is too low, you could be a risk to any mission. Why?

Let's find out from Russian space expert, Professor Karl Kosmoski.

Bill Brain: *Professor, why is low blood pressure such a problem in space?*

KOSMOSKI: Well, this is a little tricky. So why don't we start with a simple diagram of a person.

The heart pumps blood around the body. It must do so with enough force to reach the tips of your fingers and your toes, and return to be pumped out again.

On Earth, the heart has some help. Gravity pulls blood down towards your feet. And the movement of muscles in your feet and legs — including little muscles attached to veins — helps push the blood back towards your heart.

Brain: *So far, so clear, Professor.*

KOSMOSKI: But in a spacecraft, there is very little gravity. Blood is no longer pulled down towards your feet, and so those muscles in your legs have little work to do. This means they get weak. The heart also does not have to pump as hard as it does on Earth, and it too loses strength. When an astronaut returns to Earth, the heart and muscles (especially those

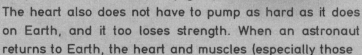

that help the leg veins) must suddenly respond to being back in normal gravity. If they're not strong enough, too little blood will reach the brain — and the astronaut will feel dizzy and could faint. Fainting is a BIG problem if the astronaut is the pilot. It could be mission over! To reduce the risk, we need to choose astronauts who have a good, strong heart, healthy vessels to carry the blood and good muscles.

Taking your blood pressure is straightforward. A nurse will use an inflatable strip of fabric round your arm to measure the maximum pushing pressure of your heart and the pressure in your blood vessels when your heart is relaxed.

Russian cosmonauts also have to have another rather more unpleasant type of blood-pressure measure. It's more complicated and it's got a name to match: *the orthostatic test.*

If you take the orthostatic test, you'll be strapped on to a movable table that will tip you up and down until you almost pass out! This will help the doctors check how well your heart and blood vessels respond to being turned and tilted. And this will give them a better idea of who is likely to become dizzy when they come back to Earth from space.

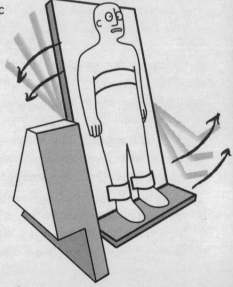

Heart and lungs

Astronauts must be supremely fit – with a powerful heart and good lungs. Running, swimming, cycling and other kinds of sweat-spurting exercise make your heart more efficient at pumping blood. Because your straining muscles need a lot of extra oxygen, exercise also means your body gets better at transferring oxygen from your lungs into your blood.

So, during fitness tests, doctors will:

1. *Check your blood pressure.*
2. *Monitor your breathing and the amount of oxygen you use.*
3. *Attach electrodes to your chest to measure the electrical activity of your heart.*

Selection doctors will expect you to turn up in very good shape. So make sure you are super-fit. If you want to be an astronaut and don't like sport, search for some kind of hard exercise you enjoy.

Hearing and vision

Ask a couple of friends to have a conversation while you stand two metres away, with your back turned. Can you hear what they're saying? If you can't, you might not pass the astronaut hearing test.

Bill Brain's Top Tips: ———————
Make sure they're not whispering!

Doctors will also peer into your eyes to check they're healthy.

Muscle strength

Space doctors have machines that can pick out individual muscles for testing. To test the strength of your arms, you'll be strapped in a chair tightly and asked to push or pull against a bar. This will help the doctors measure the strength of certain arm muscles. No one will expect you to look like Arnold Schwarzenegger, but you will have to be strong.

Bill Brain's Top Tips: ————————————————
Strong finger muscles from playing computer games or hitting the TV remote control will not count. ————————————————

Brain function

Doctors will take scans to make sure your brain is working normally.

Bill Brain's Top Tips: ————————————————
Don't listen to your friends, it probably is!

Testing, testing and even more testing ...

Now for the real fun!

Your heart's strong, your muscles check out, you can see further than the end of your nose ... But can you spin round at top speed without passing out – or throwing up?

Think of the kind of fairground ride that sends your car spinning. Remember the pressure you felt on your body as you were pushed to the back of your seat? Remember trying to scream – but you couldn't? Did you promise never to put yourself through such a sickening experience ever again? If you did, you're in trouble if you want to be an astronaut. In fact, even if you love fast-spinning fairground rides, you're in for a surprise. Because they're nothing compared with their mean big brothers ...

The centrifuge

Every would-be astronaut has to take a spin in the centrifuge. This is a small capsule on the end of a long arm that whizzes round inside a huge room hundreds of times every minute. The faster you spin, the greater the pressure on your body. The point of the test is to simulate the pressure that astronauts have to handle during take-off. To pass, all you have to do is stay conscious.

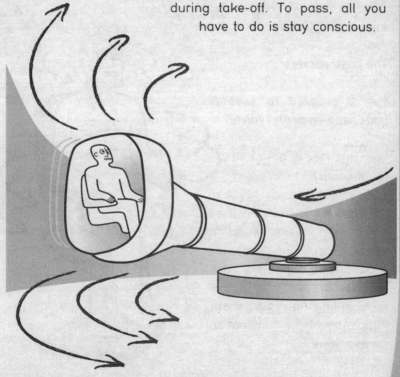

The 'vomit chair'

Vomiting is an important part of becoming an astronaut. As you'll find out, there's more than one gadget designed to push your insides until they can take it no longer. But if you get on the Russian space programme, all candidate cosmonauts need to spend time in the vomit chair.

This is how it works ...

You meet a nice Russian scientist who smiles and chats – in English, because he knows you're yet to master his language. He attaches wires to your chest and then he invites you to sit down. You've had a tough day and you're ready for a rest. But before you know it ...

You're strapped in.

The chair rotates.

You're ordered to swivel your head back and forth!

Yes, this test is designed to measure how your body's balance systems will respond to being in the weird, weightless world of space. Throw up (and it's tricky not to) and the chances are you'll be prone to vomiting in your craft. Which could be unpleasant for everyone ...

Survive all that and you're doing well. But there's no time to rest. Being in good physical shape is just the beginning. Any astronaut must also be strong in the head.

For a start, you'll be sharing your bedroom, your free time, your meals – everything, in fact, with the rest of the crew.

If a fellow astronaut loves opera music turned up full volume, there's no place to hide from it. If his second favourite pastime is singing out-of-tune love songs to a picture of his girlfriend, you'll have to learn to like it. Or at least put up with it. Failing that, save your put-downs till you're back on firm ground. Chances are you'll get used to it.

Because before anyone is passed as fit to fly, they've had a thorough mental going-over. No one, especially not you, wants to discover you're an aggressive type who hates small spaces while you're whizzing round in orbit in a tiny pressurized can. So this is where the psychologists come in. They test to see if you'll cope mentally with anything space travel might throw at you, as well as making sure you can work well as part of a team.

Think you'd be up to it mentally? Then try the quick quiz on the next page to find out ...

1. The thought of being sealed for a week in a cramped room with only water, reconstituted food and a few strange-speaking, foreign 'friends' for company makes you:

(a) excited beyond belief?

(b) scream (maths homework would be more fun)?

2. Your teacher asks your class to read out the answers to your homework. The girl next to you has her book open and you can see her answers are different from yours. When it's your turn, do you:

(a) trust your own work and read out your answers?

(b) go with hers — she's clever and she's bound to be right?

3. You asked your mum for a guitar for your birthday. You've had it six months. Can you:

(a) manage a couple of chords?

(b) play along to music by your favourite band?

4. You tell your dad you want to be an astronaut when you're older. He says you'd be better getting your head out of the clouds and aiming for a real job. Do you:

(a) accept he's probably right and think about a different career?

(b) work every day towards achieving your goal?

5. A friend asks for help with their geography homework. You understand the question and explain it as simply, patiently and clearly as you can. Do you think they'd:

(a) now understand and be able to do their homework?

(b) still be completely in the dark?

6. Your teacher sets you a project that you can complete either on your own or with two classmates. Do you:

(a) choose to do it on your own — it'll be easier?

(b) decide you'll do better if you get other people's ideas?

Answers

1. *(a)*. Obviously, if your answer is *(b)*, space travel's not for you!

2. *(a)*. Astronauts must be able to rely on their own judgement. If you're not sure of the answer, you must be able to ask for help. If you know you're right, go with it, no matter what other people say.

3. *(b)*. Sticking with something new or difficult — showing perseverance — is an essential quality of any astronaut. You'll never make it through astronaut training without it.

4. *(b)*. If someone offers you sensible advice, listen to it. But if you have what you think is an achievable goal, never let others put you off. If you do, you will never make the astronaut grade.

5. *(a)*. Good communication skills are very important for an astronaut. If you don't feel you're good at getting your thoughts across clearly, you'll need to practise.

6. *(b)*. Every astronaut is part of a team. You must be willing to work closely with others. Even if they love singing themselves to sleep!

So, do you still think you've got what it takes? If, as a candidate cosmonaut, you've passed all the tests so far, there are more. Russian space psychologists have a reputation for being the most imaginative (and that's putting it kindly) of the lot. In fact, some of their ideas sound a bit like torture!

The chamber

Do you think you could stay awake for two whole days? Yes? Then how about three? Oh, and you'll be in a sound-proof chamber with no one to talk to. And don't even think about a rest.

Imagine, after 24 hours your eyes are burning, your head's swimming, your legs are dragging you down to the floor. All day and all night you've been doing boring tasks, like sorting cards or solving sums. Think you'll take a nap? Think again! Your new instructions are coming through ...

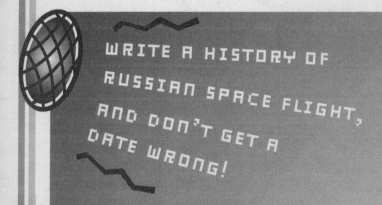

WRITE A HISTORY OF RUSSIAN SPACE FLIGHT, AND DON'T GET A DATE WRONG!

What would you do? Grab a pencil and get to it? Or would you be tempted to run to the door and let yourself out? Do that, of course, and you're out, full stop. Your hopes of being a cosmonaut are dead.

The point of the chamber test isn't to check whether you can go for long periods without sleep — or even to see how well your mind works after days awake. It's to test how much you want to succeed. To become a cosmonaut takes a lot of hard (sometimes boring) work. If you don't have the 100 per cent motivation needed to make it, it's easier to weed you out at the start, rather than to throw you off the training programme months later. Well, that's what your Russian psychologist would say.

But the Russians aren't the only ones to come up with seemingly crazy selection stunts ...

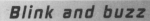

Blink and buzz

Back in the late 1950s, the NASA selectors didn't have much of an idea about who would make a great astronaut. Physical things were easy to measure. But there was something else. Something hard to pin down. Something that became known as the 'right stuff' that made a person astronaut material. To find out who had this 'right stuff', the first would-be astronauts had to pass bizarre tests. Like ...

1. Candidates wrote down who they were in 20 different ways, e.g., 'I am a girl.' 'I am a school pupil.' *(Give it a go and see how far you get.)*

2. Candidates were put into a room where they had to pull levers and push buttons to turn off blinking lights and buzzers. The test ran at normal speed for half an hour. Then suddenly it switched to double speed. This was bad enough, but after mastering double-fast lever-pulling and button-pushing, the pace increased to quadruple speed for 40 minutes. Candidates had to rush around the room, desperate to keep up, with bright lights in their eyes and buzzers screaming in their ears! The only point of the test was to see who freaked out.

3. A psychiatrist showed candidates a blank piece of paper and asked them to describe what they saw. (One candidate joked, 'It's upside-down!' He did become an astronaut — but according to reports at the time, the psychiatrist wasn't impressed.)

If you're beginning to feel that being accepted as a trainee astronaut is a lot tougher than you'd imagined, there is another option.

You won't need jet-flying time, or three times as many degrees as your teacher. You won't even have to pass all the medical and psychological tests. To be a 'space tourist' you'll need ... money. Loads of it!

NO.2 BILL BRAIN'S HALL OF ASTRO FAME

Dennis Tito
• *The first ever space tourist*

Born: 1940, USA

In May 2001, 60-year-old Dennis Tito became the first ever space tourist. Tito flew with Russian cosmonauts for an eight-day holiday on the International Space Station (ISS). High-flier Dennis had once worked at NASA as an engineer but had left to make his fortune running his own business. On his return to Earth, he said, 'It was great, best, best, best of all. It was paradise, I just came back from paradise.'

Cost of the trip: US$20 million.

When the Russians first announced Tito would be paying them to take him to the ISS, NASA wasn't pleased. It thought an amateur astronaut could put the station and its crew in danger.

So in February 2002, the countries responsible for the station, including the United States, Russia, Canada, Japan and members of the European Union, came up with a strict set of 'house rules'.

HOUSE RULES FOR TOURISTS

1. Each tourist must pass a medical examination. (This test is less strict than for real astronauts.)

2. Each tourist must undergo a minimum amount of training (to be decided on an individual basis) AND anyone staying on the International Space Station for more than a few days must train for 12 months before launch.

3. If the tourist is travelling with Russian cosmonauts, he or she must be able to speak basic Russian.

4. Criminals, drug addicts and the 'notoriously disgraceful' will not be allowed on to the ISS.

In April 2002, a South African businessman called Mark Shuttleworth became the second space tourist. And NASA agreed that tourists might eventually be allowed to stay on the station for three or four months at a time.

But to do this, they'll have to become experts at living without something YOU'RE taking for granted right now.

It rules your life and it's invisible. Ignore it and it could kill you in an instant.

Want to know more? Then turn the page to Chapter Two ...

LIVING IN MICRO G

Candidate astronaut: you're on the hunt for an invisible force that rules your life. In space you'll be without it. And without special training, you'll be in trouble.

Here are a few clues:

1. It's what makes you bash your knee hard on the ground when you trip.
2. It's why this book feels heavy in your hands.
3. It's what's stopping you floating up from your chair, bouncing against the ceiling and scaring your mum.

It's ... *gravity.*

If it weren't for gravity we'd all be floating around in space. Except that even in space, there is gravity. It's just that the effect of that gravity is very, very small. So if you hear other people talking about zero-gravity in space, you can tell them they're wrong. If you're feeling smart, you could also explain why. For that, we'll need some help from a man who died more than 275 years ago ...

(Or perhaps it should be Fall of Fame!)

Isaac Newton

· The man who discovered gravity

Born: 1642, England
Died: 1727

While sitting under a tree, an apple fell on Newton's head (or so the story goes). Instead of screaming out, as most people might, he had a bit of a breakthrough. Newton realized that a force (gravity) must have made the apple fall from the tree. He also realized that similar 'gravitational forces' must exist between all objects.

Bill Brain: Let's go over to a living (well, just about!) professor to help untangle the scientific terms. Professor Kosmoski, on the subject of gravity, perhaps you could weigh in with your thoughts.

KOSMOSKI: It will help if first we go slowly through some important terms.

Number one: FORCE. Force is simply a push or pull on an object. You can use force to open a curtain or push an old broken-down car.

Number two: MASS. The mass of an object relates to its basic make-up. Say you take two apples. They're the same in every way, except that one is twice the size of the other. Then you can say that the bigger apple has twice the mass of the smaller apple. If you took a bite out of one of those apples, it would lose some of its mass.

A living human being can never become mass-less (if you did, you'd vanish!). But you can become weightless. How?

Number three: WEIGHT. The weight of an object – like you – is actually related to the force of gravity between you and another nearby mass – say, the planet Earth.

You can walk around on the surface of Earth and not go flying off into space simply because you are a small mass (a person) very close to a really huge mass (a planet). Earth exerts a big 'gravitational pull' on you. As well as keeping you on the ground, this gravitational pull determines your weight on Earth.

If you stepped on scales in your bathroom, they might show that you weigh 30 kilograms. But what would happen if you got into a spacecraft with the scales and flew to the Moon?

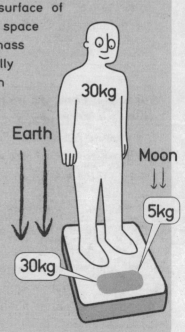

You would have exactly the same mass as on Earth. But the Moon has only one-sixth the mass of the Earth. So it would have only one-sixth of the gravitational pull of Earth on you. If you stepped on the scales, you would find that you weighed only one-sixth as much as you do in your bathroom at home (5 kilograms)!

The strength of any gravitational pull reduces quickly with distance: the farther you are from Earth, the less of its gravity you experience. Now we're really close to understanding how an astronaut can be 'weightless'.

The International Space Station is, in fact, held in a steady orbit by Earth's gravitational force.

Imagine a marble attached to the end of a piece of string and then tied to your finger. Spin the marble round. If your finger is Earth and the ISS is the marble, that piece of string represents Earth's gravitational pull.

ISS
gravity
Earth

So, you might be thinking, if the space station is held in place by Earth's gravitational pull, surely people on board should feel that gravity? Top marks for concentration! But, as you'll know if you've ever seen TV footage of astronauts on the station, they float around uncontrollably.

The reason is this: the ISS, like any spacecraft in orbit, is really in constant free-fall around Earth. And when you're free-falling, you're not in physical contact with the ground, so you feel 'weightless'.

Think you've never experienced weightlessness? Well, have you ever been in a car driving fast over a bump? Then you have. In that split second that the car was falling back after bouncing up off the road, you were weightless.

Astronauts on the ISS feel only a few millionths of the gravity you experience on Earth. Space scientists call this 'microgravity' or micro G for short.

And micro G can make things tricky for astronauts!

BILL BRAIN'S HALL OF ASTRO FAME no.4

Yuri Gagarin
• The first human in space

Born: 1934, Russia
Died: 1968

Gagarin was a brilliant fighter pilot who was among the first Russians selected for cosmonaut training. Nine years after he started training, Gagarin made history. On 12 April 1961, he became the first person to orbit the Earth. Gagarin's flight in his Vostok 1 capsule lasted just 108 minutes — enough time for him to complete only one orbit before returning to parachute down in Siberia. Tragically, he was killed before he could complete another space mission. Gagarin died when the MiG-15 fighter plane he was flying crashed near Moscow.

Although Gagarin didn't need any food for his short flight, Russian scientists wanted him to try eating and drinking, to see if it was possible in space. It was. But other tasks were a real write-off. While in orbit, Gagarin also tried to complete his log — but the pencil kept floating away. In the end, he gave up and used a tape recorder. Now anything that can float away inside a spacecraft is secured with a strip of Velcro.

Respect the law

Bill Brain: Hi folks. Here I am again with Professor Kosmoski, who is going to tell you budding astronauts about two more dangers — both of which can be explained by Newton's brilliant laws!

KOSMOSKI: Danger One — if you push off from one wall of a spacecraft, don't push too hard, because you'll keep on flying until you smack into the opposite wall!

Brain: Why, Professor?

KOSMOSKI: Well, imagine gently throwing a ball. It soon falls to the ground. This happens partly because Earth's gravity pulls it down, and partly because it is slowed by passing through the atmosphere.

But in a spacecraft, with little gravity, that ball will keep on going until it hits something. The same would be true if someone threw you!

Brain: Thanks, Professor. And the next danger?

KOSMOSKI: Danger Two — hold on to something when you sneeze!

Brain: Really?

KOSMOSKI: You might choose not to push yourself away from a wall, but you have no choice about when you sneeze. And in space, a sneeze can propel you backwards.

Brain: How?

KOSMOSKI: Well, as you sneeze, a burst of air shoots from your nose. The force of that air blasting forwards will send you flying backwards. This doesn't happen on Earth, because gravity holds you down. The same idea helps explain how a rocket launches from Earth. As the rocket blasts hot gases downwards, it shoots upwards, into space.

Bill Brain's Top Tips: _____
If you could sneeze with the same power as a rocket engine, you could launch yourself!

Phew! It might seem like a lot to take in, but microgravity isn't all hard work. Where else can you climb walls like Spider-Man, or play hide-and-seek — and hide on the ceiling? Once astronauts get used to moving around in space, most of them have a lot of fun. Those who've flown on the space shuttle say space gymnastics is very popular. Doing a triple somersault doesn't require muscles of steel when there's no gravity!

But before you get too excited about life in micro G, here's a very important warning: your body has not evolved to cope with it.

Human beings, like every animal and plant on Earth, developed to live on Earth — and under the force of Earth's gravity.

So, as well as being great to play in, micro G will do some pretty unpleasant things. It will make your face puffy, your legs spindly, your bones weak, your head dizzy and your stomach turn over.

BILL BRAIN'S ASTRO QUIZ

Try answering this question ...
Astronauts get puffy faces because:

1. They eat too much ice-cream and microgravity makes the fat settle in their cheeks instead of round their stomachs?
2. They don't sleep properly?
3. Their blood and other fluids rush to their heads and faces?

Why? Well, as you know from Chapter One, on Earth, the force of gravity pulls blood down into your legs. Your body has developed ways to cope with this — to push blood back up. But in microgravity, blood moves easily from your legs to your upper body, making your face look puffy and your legs shrink! In one day, an astronaut's legs can lose one whole litre in volume. This isn't a huge problem in space. But as you know, there's a danger that astronauts whose bodies get used to microgravity might faint when they re-enter Earth's atmosphere and blood rushes to their legs.

Can you think of a solution to the problem?

NASA has come up with several. The most interesting is a rubberized suit, called a 'G-suit', which astronauts put on for re-entry. Astronauts can inflate parts of their G-suits with air. This squeezes their arms and legs, forcing blood back towards their hearts (and so ensuring there's enough for the brain — reducing the risk of fainting).

As well as changing your body shape, that movement of fluids to the head also causes blocked noses — or 'space sniffles', as astronauts call them. So make sure you pack plenty of tissues in your space case!

Now for something that'll really turn your world upside-down — and take your stomach with it ...

On Earth, of course, you know when you're standing up straight.

Imagine a glass of water on a table. It's easy to tell if that table's on a tilt by looking at the level of the water. Your body uses the same technique.

The level of liquid in 'canals' in your inner ear provides your brain with information about your position and motion. Your brain takes that information, adds to it signals from your skin, muscles and joints, and helps you keep your balance.

Space SOS

But what's 'standing up straight' in a world with little gravity — where you can float on your head, and there's no real up or down?

In space, the balance signals from your ears and muscles go haywire, confusing your brain. The result: Space Adaptation Syndrome, SAS. Or SOS, as some astronauts might say! Because that confusion causes headaches and vomiting in about three-quarters of all people who go into space. And vomiting is a nightmare in microgravity — where sick simply floats up and away!

Remember the vomit chair on page 12? It's designed to check how bad your SAS would be.

You might be thinking micro G is more trouble than it's worth. But there's a lot more in store ...

Here's a riddle:
Where in the world can you shrink and grow at the same time?

Answer: in space!

OK, so you guessed the answer, but how?

On Earth, bones stop your body collapsing under the force of gravity. Without a skeleton, you'd be a heap on the floor. Imagine the weirdest sci-fi movie blob flopping on the ground – that would be you. Muscles help to hold up your skeleton and move it about.

But in microgravity, there's no downwards force on your body. It takes very little effort to move around, so bones and muscle lose some of their importance. Which can spell trouble for astronauts.

Bone might look dead, but it's very much alive – and regenerating all the time. Physical stress on bones is important in triggering that regeneration. In space, there's very little stress on your skeleton and, in just one month, an astronaut can lose one per cent of their amount of bone.

Tall tales

Ever wished you were taller? Well, something else strange happens during a stretch in space. In lower than normal gravity, the individual bones that make up your backbone spread out. During an average mission, you'll grow by between five and eight centimetres!

There's little that can be done to stop the gradual loss of bone – but muscles can be kept strong. How?

You've guessed it ... By regular exercise.

Of course, most of space doctors' knowledge about the effects of micro G on the body come from studies of real astronauts. Some launch with all kinds of sensors and electrodes attached to their body: 77-year-old John Glenn was one of them.

But some research into the effects of a spell in space can be done on the ground ...

European Space Agency (ESA)
VOLUNTEERS WANTED
Location: Toulouse, France
Job description:
To lie in bed for three months,
and get paid!

A joke? No! The European Space Agency really did launch a 'bedrest campaign' in 2001 and 2002. From 725 applicants, 14 people got to spend three months doing nothing but lie in bed. These people were split into roughly three equal groups. The lucky volunteers were all men, representing a range of jobs. They included a builder, a gardener, a mobile-phone salesman, a history teacher and a geography teacher (some teachers will do anything for an easy life!).

Why do you think ESA ran the experiment?

1. To find out how easily people become bored with not much to do.
2. To help them design new beds for the International Space Station.
3. To investigate the effects of little activity on the body.

Answer: 3.

Lying in bed, as you know, requires very little work. ESA's beds were tilted, so the volunteers' legs were tipped up and their heads down. This position simulated being in space – and meant doctors could keep a really close eye on the wasting effects on muscles and bones.

In fact, about 30 per cent of the volunteers were allowed to do some exercise each day. Another 30 per cent were given drugs designed to combat muscle-wasting. But the remaining third did absolutely nothing. This was so doctors could compare the results and investigate the best approach for treating real astronauts on long missions in space.

So, what happened after three months?

For all the volunteers, it was tough going. Some became so frustrated, at night they dreamed of flying – they wanted to be free as birds. And they were so weak that when they eventually took their first steps, they had to be helped by the researchers.

The doctors found that the drugs to stop muscle-wasting worked – but not as well as the exercise. That's bad news if you were hoping to take a pill to keep yourself fit in space!

BILL BRAIN'S ASTRO QUIZ

Of course, microgravity doesn't only have a strange effect on people. See if you can answer these questions:

1. What does a weightless flame look like:
(a) a glowing sphere?
(b) a spiralling spark?
(c) a pulsating mass?

2. What happens to mice in space:
(a) they panic and attack each other?
(b) they adapt very well?
(c) they roll into a ball and go to sleep?

3. How do plants grow in microgravity:
(a) just as they do on Earth?
(b) they get confused and send roots upwards and shoots down?
(c) they send out roots and shoots all over the place?

Answers:

1. *(a)* Yes, in space, a flame becomes a beautiful glowing blue sphere.

2. *(b)* Animals don't seem to mind microgravity much at all. Within about five minutes of being up there, mice start eating and grooming normally.

3. *(c)* Most plants can sense gravity. This 'tells' them where to send out roots (downwards, underground) and where to send out shoots (upwards, to the light). But in microgravity, plants become utterly confused. Roots and shoots spurt out in every direction. At least, that's true for most plants. A little plant called fire moss grows in tangled clumps on Earth. But in microgravity, it grows in neat spiral patterns — not randomly at all. Scientists are still trying to work out exactly why.

But survival is one thing. Performing properly in space requires months and months of training. Beware: only the toughest will make it through ...

CHAPTER 3

TIME TO TRAIN

It's the middle of winter in a freezing field in Siberia. You're exhausted and bone-shakingly cold. To survive, you'll have to collect wood and make a fire. You set out, dragging your feet through the snow ... But what's this? The rustle of trees. The howl of a wolf! You must defend yourself — or risk death.

Think someone's accidentally slipped the wrong pages into your book? In fact, being able to survive in the wilderness is an essential part of astronaut training. In this chapter, you'll learn why. You'll also discover what other training 'treats' your instructors have in store ...

Location, location, location

Star sailors come from all over the world. But all those that actually make it on to a mission will train in one — or both — of two locations:

JOHNSON SPACE CENTER, USA

STAR CITY, RUSSIA

NASA astronauts preparing to live on the International Space Station spend 30 weeks in Russia, training on mock-ups of the Russian components and practising their language skills. Russian cosmonauts make the trip to the USA to learn about American modules and techniques.

TRAINING FILE

- **NAME:** Johnson Space Center.
- **ESTABLISHED:** 1961, as the Manned Spacecraft Center. Renamed in 1973 in honour of President Lyndon B. Johnson.
- **LOCATION:** 2101 NASA Road 1, Houston, Texas.
- **DESCRIPTION:** Gleaming buildings and straight roads with names like Saturn Lane.
- **FACILITIES:** Include an astronaut training centre and Mission Control Center, which manages all activity on board the International Space Station and directs all shuttle missions.

TRAINING FILE

- **NAME:** Zvezdny Gorodok (Star City), home to the Yuri Gagarin Cosmonaut Training Centre.
- **LOCATION:** Zvezdny, one hour's drive north-east of Moscow.
- **DESCRIPTION:** High-rise apartment blocks surrounded by fields.
- **FACILITIES:** Include the world's biggest centrifuge – an 18-metre monster that'll spin you round till your cheeks hit your ears.

Would-be space tourists, take note: Star City will be your training destination.

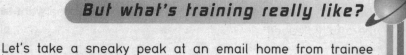

But what's training really like?

Let's take a sneaky peak at an email home from trainee American astronaut Dwight Dirkswood.

From: Dwight Dirkswood
Date: Mon Feb 4th, 16:04
To: Jean and Chuck Dirkswood
Subject: Private

Hi Mom and Dad

Arrived safely in Star City. The food's great. I just love that boiled cabbage and meatballs. But talk about pickled beetroot — you should see my face after high G training! Only joking!

This place is ginormous. There's a kindergarten, school, hotels, tennis courts, a swimming pool, even department stores, so I can replace the kit I ruin after those high-flying sessions in the vomit comet. Still can't get used to it.

In fact, gotta run ...

Back soon, your loving son,

Dwight

Now we'll take a closer look at what lies ahead if you want to be a fully fledged ...

Astronaut

BASIC TRAINING: 12 months' instruction in science, spacecraft operation, working in microgravity and survival.

ADVANCED TRAINING: Concentrating on the space shuttle and on the details of the mission you'll be flying. Trainee pilot astronauts will fly 15 hours each month in a high-performance T-38 jet. Mission specialists will fly at least four hours per month.

Space tourist

At least 12 months' training for anyone spending more than a few days on the International Space Station. You will complete much of the basic astronaut training.

Space tourists, like rookie astronauts, will have to go through classroom learning before they're let loose on the expensive equipment. You might think school is bad, but space training is even more intense.

A SPACE TOURIST'S MORNING TIMETABLE	
6.00 a.m.	Breakfast, while revising Russian.
6.45 a.m.	Fitness training – a quick 8-km jog (while practising a conversation about Moon rocks in Russian in your head).
8.00 a.m.	Physics – what makes a spacecraft shoot up from Earth and spin round it without drifting off into outer space.

10.00 a.m.	Russian language – verbs.
11.00 a.m.	Physics of a shuttle launch (more equations than you've ever seen before in your life).
12.00 p.m.	Lunch, while revising Russian.

Mission training

Think of your school's hardest-working student – and multiply by 100. That will be you during your astronaut training. You'll learn basic mathematics, oceanography, astronomy, geology and the physics of what happens in orbit round Earth ... and Russian.

Try mastering these 'easy' phrases:

ENGLISH	RUSSIAN
Hello	Zdravstvuitye!
My name is...	Menya Zavoot ...
I don't understand	Ya ne panimayoo
You are my best friend	Vi moi lyoobimi droog (boy)
	Vi moya lyoobimaya padrooga (girl)

In Star City, all non-Russian trainees learn basic Russian – essential for getting along, especially if you're in trouble. And you'll get a lot of experience of that ...

The 'vomit comet'

Imagine this: you're on the longest, fastest rollercoaster in the world. You're shooting straight down a never-ending slope. Then you're flipped on your back and you're climbing, face to the sky, getting higher and higher and higher until ... Bam! You're falling. And you're climbing and falling over and over and over again.

The most extreme funfair ride?
Hideous torture?
No ... It's worse!

The idea of the vomit comet is to simulate what it would be like in space. You'll step into a modified jet plane, which climbs to between 7,000 and 10,000 metres and then drops suddenly. The freefall lasts about 30 seconds, before the plane shoots back up, only to drop again ...

During the freefall, you'll be in microgravity, and you'll be able to practise some essential space skills – like not throwing up! Most trainee astronauts are sick during their first few flights, but gradually they get used to this extreme form of motion sickness.

Sadly for trainee astronauts, long periods of microgravity on Earth just aren't possible. But there is a way to mimic it for more than 30 seconds, to give astronauts a real chance to practise their space moves. Can you guess what it is?

1. *Hanging upside-down?*
2. *Being submerged in water?*
3. *Lying in bed?*

Answer: 2.
As you know, being in bed does simulate some of the effects of microgravity on the body – but it doesn't help astronauts train for moving about in weightlessness.

Hanging upside-down will make the blood rush to your head, but you'll still feel and see that force of gravity, especially if you have long hair!

The closest we can get to weightlessness on Earth, outside the vomit comet, is moving about in a giant tank of water. That's because the water supports your body evenly and reduces the sensation of gravity. If you're a really good swimmer, try doing a somersault under water next time you're in a pool – and you'll get a feel for what it would be like to do a somersault in space.

DID YOU KNOW?

French choreographer Kitsou Dubois thinks dance training could help trainee astronauts adjust to micro G, and reduce space sickness. Dubois has created a series of moves to improve awareness of the position of your arms and legs. This also shows how certain movements might affect your balance. She recommends pelvis and upper body rotations, leaps and bends and walking with weights tied round your waist.

NAME: Neutral Buoyancy Laboratory.
LOCATION: Star City.
DIMENSIONS: 23 metres diameter.
DEPTH: 12 metres.
CAPACITY: 5 million litres.

NAME: Neutral Buoyancy Laboratory.
LOCATION: Johnson Space Center.
DIMENSIONS: 31 metres wide, 62 metres long.
DEPTH: 12 metres.
CAPACITY: 23 million litres.

As a trainee astronaut, you first have to pass a swimming test (three lengths of a 25-metre pool in a flight suit and trainers, plus ten minutes treading water). And you have to learn to scuba dive.

Then, you'll be allowed into the vast swimming pool wearing modified spacesuits – or Extra-vehicular Mobility Units, as NASA calls them (see page 86). Each suit weighs about 100 kilograms. That's more than twice your bodyweight. Luckily special cranes are on hand to lower suited-up astronauts into the pool.

Once in the pool, you'll get a feel for moving around in space, and for doing space walks alongside mock-ups of parts of the ISS.

Air and power get to the spacesuit through hoses and cables. And air 'envelopes' on the suit's chest, hands and legs help the astronaut maintain 'neutral buoyancy'. All that means is staying in one position, and not sinking or floating up to the surface. By adding more air to the pockets, you'll rise. Letting air out will make you sink.

Floating about in a giant swimming pool might seem a breeze after the vomit comet. But don't relax just yet ...

Going for a spin

As part of your astronaut training you'll take a few turns in a monster centrifuge (like the one used in the selection tests). You'll be escorted to your capsule at the end of a huge metal arm, strapped in and spun so fast your stomach will squirm. The point? To prepare your body for the forces it will feel during take-off. According to space experts, practice will help you to cope.

Working out

Yes, we're back to physical exercise. As you know, moving about in space takes a lot less effort than on Earth. To keep your muscles in good shape, you'll need to bulk them up before you leave. Running, swimming, cycling and dancing are all excellent ways to build muscle and to get fit.

Bill Brain's Note: _____
You cannot avoid the punishing workout schedule. If you're not super fit now, by the time you leave Star City, you will be. _____

Survival training

All wannabe astronauts will also have to make parachute jumps. Officially, it's in case your returning NASA shuttle develops a fault and you have to bail out. But NASA will admit it's also to keep astronauts in the right mental state: ready for anything, ready to take a controlled risk.

Being ready for anything also means being ready for returning from space to anywhere on Earth. Unlike NASA's shuttle, the Russian Soyuz capsule doesn't land like a plane. Although it usually drifts down by parachute to a pre-chosen spot on the land, it could also land in the sea — or in the middle of the Sahara, or the Arctic.

Coping with space is hard. But coping with burning sands and scorching sun, or killer cold and unfriendly polar bears, is also dangerous — if you're unprepared.

The Big Chill

As part of your training, you'll be abandoned in one of the coldest parts of the world for a few days, with only a hard-hearted instructor for company.

Think you'd be hot at keeping out the cold? Then check your chilly survival skills with this quiz.

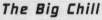

BILL BRAIN'S ASTRO QUIZ

1. You're very cold and your matches are soggy. What's the best way to warm up?

(a) jump up and down and work up a sweat?

(b) curl up in a ball and use as little energy as possible?

(c) unzip your clothes and run on the spot for five minutes?

2. You're thirsty. The best thing to do is:

(a) eat snow?

(b) melt snow and drink it?

(c) find a stone and put it in your mouth — it will reduce your feeling of thirst?

3. Your fingers have gone numb and are starting to turn black. You should:

(a) rub them?

(b) clap your hands?

(c) tuck them in your armpits?

Answers:

1. *(c).* Sweating makes you lose heat — so it's the last thing you want to do. If you unzip your jacket and jump up and down or jog, you should warm yourself up without sweating too much.

2. *(b).* If possible, don't eat snow: it's so cold, it'll chill you right down. Try to melt snow first, perhaps by collecting it in a plastic bag and holding that bag in the sun.

3. *(c.)* If your fingers or toes are turning black, the chances are you have frostbite. This happens when you get so cold, your body tries to keep heat inside by reducing supply to your skin. Without oxygen, the skin and then the flesh start to die. If you rub a badly frost-bitten finger, you might cause even more damage. Instead, hold it against hotter parts of your body, like your armpits, to help stop that frostbite spreading.

Other things you'll learn during your training are:

HOW TO BUILD A SHELTER USING ONLY WHAT YOU CAN FIND AROUND YOU.

Bill Brain's Top Tips: _____
You'll have a knife in your emergency pack, so you should be able to cut down branches and leaves. If you're in a snowy wasteland, you'll need to gather snow to form a barrier against the wind. You could even dig out a shelter for yourself from an icy mountainside. Remember: native Alaskan people didn't build icy igloos because they like the cold! _____

HOW TO START A FIRE.

Bill Brain's Top Tips: _____
You should also have matches in your pack. Find the driest leaves and smallest twigs to start your fire, but keep a stash of dry branches close by. Make sure your fuel is sheltered from wind — if this is difficult, try using three matches at once for extra 'firepower'. Blow gently to get the flames going. Then add your branches. You should be toasty in no time. _____

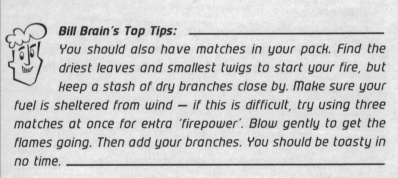

Desert survival

But what if you landed right in the middle of a blistering hot desert? Then, you'll need to know all about how to keep your cool in the heat. One of your most important tasks will be to find water — or to collect it. How might you do it?

1. Find a cactus and drink the liquid inside?
Only drink liquid from a cactus if you KNOW it's a type
that's safe. Liquid from some cactuses will burn your
throat and stomach – and could kill you long before you
would die of thirst.

**2. Dig a hole in the ground, put a cup in it and cover the
hole with a piece of plastic with a stone on top?**
This technique should work well if you have the right
equipment. But you'll have to wait until the morning for your
water. As the sun begins to heat the ground, dew will form
on the underside of your piece of plastic. The weight of the
stone will channel the dew so that it drips right into your cup.

**3. Look for animal tracks and follow them to the closest
water-hole?**
Not a good bet. The animal tracks could be going anywhere
– and there's no guarantee they'll lead you to water.

Sea survival

Astronaut training will really push you to the extremes.
As well as learning how to cope in terrible cold and deadly
heat, you'll be pushed out of a plane into the sea ...

- -

Dwight Dirkswood, Space Log.
Earth Date: 12 February

Day started well with a breakfast of sausage and
toast (got to keep my energy up!), then it was off
to the Black Sea to be pushed out in a mock-up of

the Soyuz capsule. Almost brought those sausages back up as we bounced around on the waves – but at last I managed to get the capsule door open and set off the flares! Had to swim to the rescue ship and they hauled me on board. Talk about cold – even my stomach was shivering! Though I guess that could have been the seasickness ...

Flight training

After a stretch of survival training, it's back indoors for some real fun. Now's your chance to fly in a spacecraft! Well ... a simulator. Both Star City and NASA have their own spacecraft simulators. Let's take a closer look at NASA's.

TRAINING FILE

NAME: Shuttle Mission Simulator (SMS).
LOCATION: Building 5, Johnson Space Center.
BUILT: 1977 (and constantly updated).
COST: US$100 million.

After training with an instructor, who'll tell you how to operate the shuttle and how to deal with emergencies, you'll be let loose on the SMS. This hi-tech simulator replicates exactly every single aspect of a shuttle mission from 30 minutes before blast-off. It's fitted with controls, displays and consoles identical to those found in a real shuttle. You'll hear and feel thrusters firing, vibrations, mechanical valves opening and closing and touchdown. Everything looks, feels and sounds just like the real thing.

Four systems create digital scenes to match the sound and sensations. In the six windows before you, you'll see the Earth, Sun, Moon and stars — while the bright International Space Station grows ever closer. Or you might see the emergency lights flash and hear a terrible alarm indicating the pressure inside your shuttle is dropping. SMS instructors can set off 6,800 different 'malfunction simulations' to prepare astronauts for every emergency. In fact, many astronauts have reported feeling no fear during their first real take-off, because the experience was so familiar, and they felt trained to deal with any emergency.

As a trainee astronaut, you'll have to spend more than 300 hours simulating launch, ascent, orbit, rendezvous with the International Space Station, docking, undocking, re-entry, approach to Earth, landing and more.

Think you're ready?

Then keep your eyes open: in the rest of this book you'll pick up top training tips to help you become a real space traveller.

CHAPTER 4
LIFT OFF!

Think you'd like fast living?

Well, life doesn't get any faster than sitting in a spacecraft strapped to giant rockets and blasting off to reach 28,000 km/h just eight and a half minutes after leaving the launch pad.

That's ...

- *80 times faster than a Formula 1 racing car*

  - *11 times faster than Concorde*

    - *9 times faster than a rifle bullet*

      - *8 times faster than the world's fastest fighter plane*

Bill Brain: *Here I am talking to astronaut Dwight Dirkswood. Dwight, what's it like to blast off in a space shuttle?*

- - - - - - - - - - - - - - - - - - - -

Dwight: Well, Bill, it's rough. Those first two minutes before the solid boosters drop off are a hell of a shaky ride. Then the push from the engines feels like it is right up against your seat. But hey, I've trained for this more times than I've had steak and salsa, and I hear there's a lot of that on board the ISS. Can't wait!

But for a better idea of what actually happens during launch, we'll need to take a closer look at the space shuttle.

The space shuttle

The shuttle has more than 2.5 million parts. But it has three main components: the orbiter, solid rocket boosters and external tank.

Orbiter

LENGTH: 37.24 metres
HEIGHT: 17.25 metres
WINGSPAN: 23.79 metres
WEIGHT (EMPTY): 75,000 kilograms

This is the plane-shaped part of the shuttle that carries the astronauts and whatever cargo – or payload – they may be taking up with them. On return to Earth, the pilot must safely glide the orbiter to a landing.

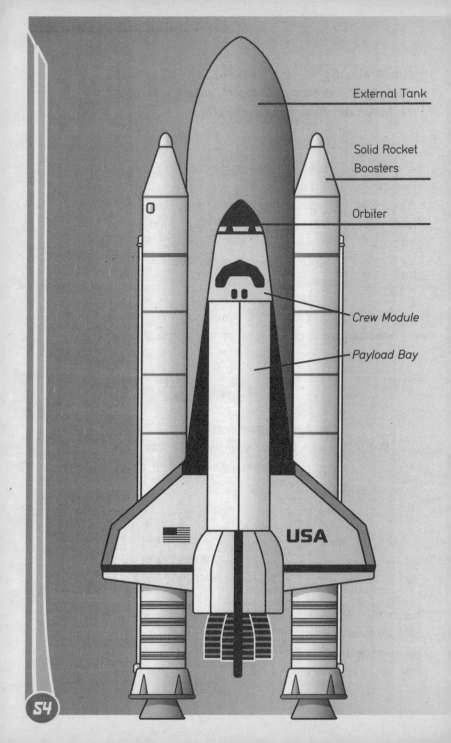

External Tank

Solid Rocket
Boosters

Orbiter

Crew Module

Payload Bay

USA

The **crew module**, which can carry up to eight astronauts, is to the front of the orbiter. Behind it is the payload bay, which is 18 metres long and 4.5 metres across.

The frame of the orbiter is made from aluminium – the same kind of metal used for soft-drink cans. But its skin is covered with heat-resistant materials, including huge heat-proof 'blankets', and more than 24,000 silica tiles. You wouldn't want to cover your own roof with them because these tiles cost up to US$4,000 each! They are tough enough to withstand horrific temperatures during re-entry into Earth's atmosphere. These temperatures, particularly on the forward edges of the wings, can soar as high as 1,600°C.

As you've probably guessed, the windows of the cockpit aren't made from your usual kind of house-window glass. They are specially strengthened to withstand the heat of re-entry and the pressure inside the shuttle, and to deflect any debris that might hit them.

Solid Rocket Boosters

The space shuttle has two. These boosters burn solid fuel during the first two minutes after launch. Most of that fuel is powdered aluminium. Once the fuel has been used up, the boosters fall away and parachute down to the ocean. Recovery teams collect them, repair them and refill them for the next launch.

External Tank

This enormous fuel tank supplies super-cold liquid hydrogen fuel and oxygen to the orbiter's three main engines during the launch and ascent. The main waste product from the combustion is water, which spurts away as steam. This tank is also jettisoned when its fuel is used up. It burns up.

Together, the shuttle's three main engines have an equivalent of 37 million horsepower (which really does mean the combined power of 37 million horses!). Each engine uses enough fuel to fill a large swimming pool every 25 seconds.

DID YOU KNOW?

1. A shuttle rocket booster is about the same height as the Statue of Liberty.
2. Gases are pushed out of the base of the rocket booster at about five times the speed of sound.

NASA has three shuttles in active service:

1. **Discovery** (built 1983). Named after two ships. The first was captained by Henry Hudson on an expedition to locate a short cut through North America from the Atlantic to the Pacific Oceans. (He didn't find one.) The second was sailed by James Cook when he discovered Hawaii.

2. **Endeavour** (built 1991). Named after James Cook's first ship, which discovered and mapped the eastern coast of

Australia and New Zealand. Endeavour replaced the shuttle Challenger, which blew up shortly after launch in January 1986. Challenger was also named after a research ship.

3. Atlantis (built 1985): Named after ...

(a) *the mysterious lost undersea city, popular with movie-makers and TV documentary crews?*

(b) *a US sailing ship used to study the oceans between 1930 and 1966?*

Answer: (b). Yes, no doubt you've already spotted the shuttle-naming pattern. Names of old ships are top of NASA's list!

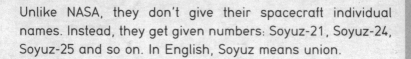

But what about the Russians?

Unlike NASA, they don't give their spacecraft individual names. Instead, they get given numbers: Soyuz-21, Soyuz-24, Soyuz-25 and so on. In English, Soyuz means union.

The first Soyuz flew in 1967. The latest version, the Soyuz TMA, blasted off in October 2002. It also doubles as the escape capsule on the International Space Station. It has been modified to take tall people – such as lanky NASA astronauts – to and from the ISS.

The Soyuz can take three cosmonauts, and it is not reusable like the shuttle.

Confusingly, the rocket that launches it has the same name. So if anyone asks if you fancy a ride into space in a Soyuz, you'd better make sure they mean the capsule!

Soyuz TMA

LENGTH: 7.5 metres
LIVING AREA: 9 square metres
WEIGHT: 7,250 kilograms

As you can see, the Soyuz has three main modules: the Orbital Module, the Re-entry Module and the Service Module.

Orbital module ——————

This contains the air-purification system, the toilet, the docking mechanism and the hatch through which cosmonauts pass to enter another craft, such as the International Space Station.

Re-entry module ——————

This contains seats for two or three cosmonauts, the control panel, the life-support systems, the basic navigation systems and a TV camera. This is the only part of a Soyuz

craft that returns to Earth. The module is fitted with a parachute to provide a soft landing (at least that's the idea), and
a periscope to give cosmonauts a view of Earth's surface as
they descend.

Service module

This contains thrusters that control the spacecraft's altitude
and its approach on docking. It also contains the radio communications antenna and the solar panel attachment. The
solar panels have a span of 10.7 metres and deliver addi-
tional electrical power to the spacecraft.

All three modules remain connected until the cosmonauts are
ready to return to Earth *(technical term: de-orbit)*. As the craft
moves out of its orbit, the modules separate. The Orbit Module
and the Service Module fall away and burn up in Earth's
atmosphere, while the Re-entry Module shoots towards
Earth's surface.

The Soyuz crew usually consists of:

THE COMMANDER, in the centre seat
THE FLIGHT ENGINEER, in the left-hand seat
THE COSMONAUT-RESEARCHER, in the right-hand seat

All Soyuz missions blast off from the Baikonur Cosmodrome in Kazakhstan, Central Asia. This launch site spreads over 6,717 square kilometres and it is the largest in the world.

But did you know that the Baikonur Cosmodrome is not actually in Baikonur, which is a real mining town in Kazakhstan. In fact, it's about 320 kilometres away. The former Soviet Union called it Baikonur Cosmodrome to disguise its true location. The secret is now out — but the name has stuck.

If you're a bit of a geography whiz, you might be confused right now — Kazakhstan is far from Moscow! Some 2,100 kilometres south-east, in fact. So why there? And why has NASA decided to launch from the Kennedy Space Center in Florida?

These locations were no accident. They were carefully chosen.

Bill Brain: Professor, can you tell us why these places were chosen?

KOSMOSKI: Imagine that you are spinning a football on your finger. Now imagine a line drawn horizontally round the biggest part of the bulge. This bulging part is actually spinning faster than the top and bottom of the ball. And the same is true for Earth. Earth is spinning constantly, and it spins fastest round its equator. So, when it comes to picking a launch site, you want to be as close to the equator as possible, because the extra spin helps the spacecraft on its way.

KAZAKHSTAN

FLORIDA

Equator

So for NASA, Florida, in the far south of the USA, is about as close as they can get to the equator. And the same was true for Kazakhstan in the old USSR. When Soviet space officials were looking for a launch spot, they chose Baikonur, which is much closer to the equator than Moscow (and has much more space).

After the USSR broke up into separate countries, Russia had to start paying Kazakhstan to use the cosmodrome.

Countdown!

But what about the timing of launches? When so much is at stake, timing is everything. For a space-shuttle launch, the countdown starts three days before blast-off is scheduled — that's three days before the 'launch window'.

To rendezvous with the International Space Station, a shuttle is always launched so that its flight path will be as short as possible. The time for a launch for the shortest flight might be only a few minutes. This is called the 'launch window'. If the shuttle blasts off outside the 'window', it might not have enough fuel to reach the ISS.

The countdown begins ...

T–3 DAYS (that's launch time minus three days)
- The entire launch team assembles in the Firing Room of the Launch Control Center at Kennedy Space Center.
- Power starts flowing to the space shuttle.
- Controllers check back-up flight systems.

T–2 DAYS
- The different sections inside the orbiter are checked and its navigational systems are tested.
- The fuel-cell storage tanks start to be filled. These tanks hold the oxygen and hydrogen that are used to create electricity on board the shuttle.

T–1 DAY
- Engineers conduct final preparations on the three main engines. (They don't add the fuel yet. It's safer to keep all that flammable material away from the shuttle for as long as possible.)
- Flight controls and navigational and communications systems are switched on.

LAUNCH DAY
On launch day itself, astronauts, engineers and mission control make their final preparations ...

The final countdown

T–6 HRS
- Propellant loaded into the external tank.

T–2 HRS 55 MINS
- Flight crew departs for launch pad.

T−2 HRS 30 MINS
* Flight crew enters orbiter.

T−20 MINS
* Orbiter computers are configured for launch.

T−9 MINS
* Ground launch sequencer is started.

T−7 MINS 30 SECS
* Access arm attached to orbiter is removed.

T−5 MINS
* Shuttle pilot starts auxiliary power units.

T−3 MINS 30 SECS
* Orbiter switches to internal power.

T−2 MINS 55 SECS
* Liquid oxygen tank pressurizes for flight.

T−1 MIN 57 SECS
* Liquid hydrogen tank pressurizes.

T−31 SECS
* Orbiter computers start the automatic launch sequence.

T−28 SECS
* Single rocket booster hydraulic power units active.

T−6 SECS
* Main engines start.

T−3 SECS
* Main engines at 90 per cent thrust.

T−0
* Rocket booster ignition and lift off!

(At T+7 seconds, control switches to Mission Control at the Johnson Space Center.)

They're off!

Oribiting the Earth in a shuttle, you'll be able to see objects as small as 150 metres across. So you will be able to see the Great Wall of China, as well as the pyramids in Egypt. And if you're lucky, you'll be able to watch one of the greatest shows ever: lightning storms on the continents way below. From your space-shuttle window, you'll also watch stars shining – and another bright glow, the gleam of the International Space Station.

BILL BRAIN'S HALL OF ASTRO FAME no.5

William M. Shepherd
· The first Commander of the ISS

Born: 1949, USA

William Shepherd served with one of the US Navy's Underwater Demolition Teams and with other elite naval forces before being selected to train as an astronaut in 1984.
On 31 October 2000, he became the first-ever Commander of the International Space Station.

International Space Station (ISS)

The hottest destination in space! In fact, the only realistic space destination – apart from maybe the Moon. If you're blasting off, the likelihood is you'll be staying in orbit in your shuttle or Soyuz, or heading here, to humankind's own star of the sky.

DISTANCE FROM EARTH: 400 kilometres
FIRST MODULE LAUNCHED: 1998
ARRIVAL OF FIRST SEMI-PERMANENT CREW: 2000

Recent budget cuts at NASA and ongoing financial troubles at the Russian Space Agency mean the ISS might not end up quite as big as its designers had imagined (larger than a five-bedroomed house). But if it is finally fully completed, these will be its vital statistics:

NUMBER OF MAIN COMPONENTS: more than 100
NUMBER OF SPACE FLIGHTS NEEDED TO DELIVER THE COMPONENTS: 44
NUMBER OF SPACEWALKS NEEDED TO ASSEMBLE IT: 160
TOTAL LENGTH WHEN COMPLETE: 110 metres
PROJECTED LIFESPAN: 10 years
PROJECTED COST: US$37 billion
PROJECTED COMPLETION DATE: 2006

When finished, the ISS will appear in the night sky about as bright as the planet Venus. It will be home for up to seven astronauts for between three and seven months at a time.

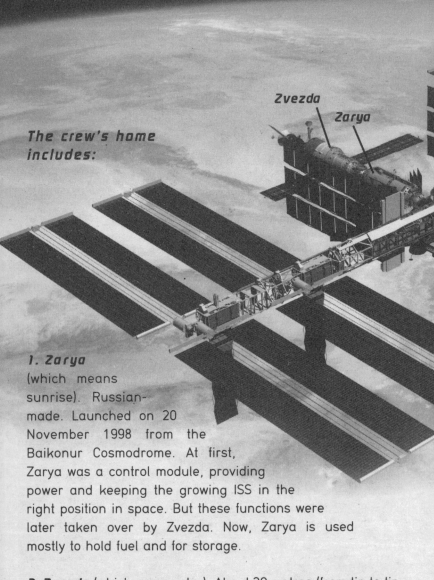

Zvezda

Zarya

The crew's home includes:

1. Zarya
(which means
sunrise). Russian-
made. Launched on 20
November 1998 from the
Baikonur Cosmodrome. At first,
Zarya was a control module, providing
power and keeping the growing ISS in the
right position in space. But these functions were
later taken over by Zvezda. Now, Zarya is used
mostly to hold fuel and for storage.

2. Zvezda (which means star). About 30 metres (from tip to tip
of the solar panels) by 13 metres. Russian-made. Launched
in July 2000 from the Baikonur Cosmodrome, it contains living
quarters where the crew eat, sleep, exercise, go to the toilet

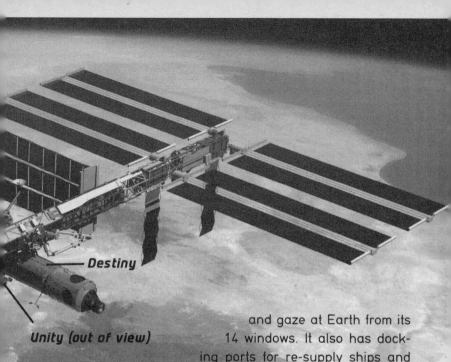

Destiny

Unity (out of view)

and gaze at Earth from its 14 windows. It also has docking ports for re-supply ships and rocket engines to keep the ISS in orbit. Russian Soyuz and the unmanned Progress cargo ships can dock with Zvezda.

3. Unity. US-made. 4.5 metres by 5.5 metres. Launched in December 1998 from the Kennedy Space Center. The first of three 'connector' modules, it has six ports and is designed to help hold the space station together, as well as to carry fluid, electricity and data to other modules attached to it. The shuttle docks with Unity.

4. Destiny. US-made. 8.5 metres by 4.3 metres. Launched in February 2001 from the Kennedy Space Center. Experiments in medicine, engineering, physics, biotechnology and other sciences are planned for this hi-tech laboratory module.

So that's the layout.

BILL BRAIN'S ASTRO QUIZ

Space-rocket scientists have some of the most knowledgeable scientific brains in the world. But a lack of knowledge doesn't stop other people having a go. See how much of a rocket whizz you are by taking this quick quiz.

1. The first rocket-powered weapons were built in:

(a) America?

(b) China?

(c) Russia?

(d) India?

2. The first rocket-powered form of transportation was a:

(a) bathtub?

(b) chariot?

(c) chair?

(d) horse?

3. The first-ever rocket-like device was built in:

(a) 1960?

(b) 400 BC?

(c) 1918?

(d) AD 10?

Answers:

1. (b). In the first century AD, the Chinese filled short bamboo tubes with an explosive mix of saltpetre, sulphur and charcoal dust. But the first records of their use in battle date from 1232. Then Chinese warriors at war with the Mongols capped one end of a tube and

shoved in a gunpowder mix. They attached the tubes to long sticks. When they lit the powder, fire, smoke and gas burst out of the open end and sent the 'fire arrow' shooting towards the enemy.

2. (c). An old Chinese legend tells how an official called Wan-Hu was the first to attempt rocket-powered motion. He attached 47 fire arrows to 47 kites, and attached these kites to a chair. Assistants lit the arrows with torches and stood back ... Clouds of smoke filled the air. And when they cleared, Wan-Hu and the chair had disappeared.

Bill Brain's Note: _____
If this story is true, most scientists think Wan-Hu simply blew himself and the chair to pieces, rather than flew off! _____

3. (b). According to ancient Roman writings, a Greek man called Archytas of Tarentum built the earliest rocket-like device in 400 BC. If a scrap of verse describing the 'magical' construction remained, this is how it might read:

'My friends, I sing to you tonight
Of a wooden bird — engaged in flight!
A bird on wires! A bird that zoomed!
That swept 'cross Archytas' living room!
I swear to you — 'twas not a dream —
That lifeless pigeon farted steam!'

That's right — the earliest recorded rocket-like device was a wooden pigeon suspended on wires, propelled by steam power.

CHAPTER 5

LIVING IN SPACE

Are you an extremely neat, clean kind of person?
Do you enjoy precision-brushing your teeth?
Scrubbing behind your ears every morning?
Do you throw out a T-shirt if you splash a stain
down the front?

No??

Then space is the place for you! No baths, for a start. And you'll have to wear your clothes for days before changing them. You'll slurp your food and you'll sleep where you like. Oh, and you'll drink tea made from urine.

Yes, in this chapter, you'll discover all the dirty details about life in space ...

Think about an ordinary Monday morning. Let's say you get out of bed, have a shower, get dressed, eat breakfast, go to school ... Of course, you can forget about the school part in space. But you'll need to attempt the rest.

First, a shower ...

The International Space Station version wouldn't win any power-shower awards on Earth. In a shower at home, you'll use about 50 litres of water. On the ISS, you'll get just four.

You'll step into its tiny shower unit, and water squirted out of the 'top' will trickle over you and be sucked in by fans at the 'bottom'.

Alternatively, you might choose just to wash your body and face. No running a tap into a sink, though. You'll have to spray a little water on a cloth and use that.

Then, a trip to the loo ...

What about going to the toilet?

Holding it in for the two-day trip on the shuttle to the ISS just won't be possible. But the space-shuttle toilet – otherwise known as the Waste Collection System (WCS) – isn't an attractive option either. You'd have to be a loo-natic to want to use it.

The shuttle toilet is very similar to the ISS version. It's slotted into a tiny room, about 75 centimetres wide.

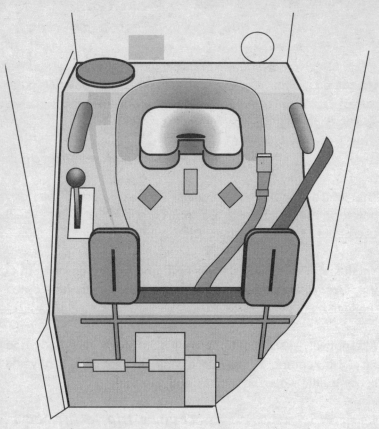

To take a pee, whether you're male or female, you'll use a funnel attached to a hose. You can use this while sitting on the toilet or standing.

The system works a bit like a vacuum cleaner, drawing in urine and air to a rotating tank. Here, the urine/air mix is spun, forcing the liquid outwards to a waste-water tank.

Bill Brain's Top Tips: ─────────────────
Don't practise with the vacuum at home!

But what if you need to pass something more solid?

Bill Brain: Here I am back with Professor Kosmoski. Professor, how does a shuttle toilet work?

KOSMOSKI: First, you sit down on the toilet. A metal bar and four Velcro straps go over your legs to stop you floating away.

The toilet seat is a little squidgy, so there are no gaps between it and your buttocks. This prevents any little bits from escaping! Then, air sucked in from the cabin pushes your poo towards the bottom of the toilet and into a bag. This bag collects all the solid waste, but it lets the air pass through it. When you are finished, you press a lever to open a valve and the waste is sucked away into drums for disposal.

Solid toilet waste isn't dumped straight into space. It's either returned to Earth on the shuttle or it's collected from the ISS using an unmanned Russian Progress cargo ship. This hugely expensive garbage truck burns up with all its contents on re-entering Earth's atmosphere.

Freezing sight

Urine is not stored for long on the shuttle. And when the waste-water tank is emptied, it produces a golden, frozen stream. It might sound revolting, but this is what astronaut Russell Schweickart had to say:

> 'One of the most beautiful sights is a urine dump at sunset. As the stuff comes out and as it hits the exit nozzle, it instantly flashes into 10 million little ice crystals ... a spray of sparkles. It's a really spectacular sight.'

On the ISS, no water of any kind is wasted. Go to the toilet here and the following day you could find yourself drinking your own urine – along with somebody else's sweat ...

The ISS was designed to be brilliant at recycling. When it costs a small fortune to ship up enough water for one smelly astronaut to take a shower, it's no wonder that water is recycled as much as possible.

But cost isn't the only consideration. When you breathe out, you put moisture into the air. When you sweat, that sweat evaporates into the air. The same goes for any lab animals that might be on the ISS.

But too much water in the air – too much humidity – can be dangerous, because the excess water could condense and ruin vital equipment. It's also a little unpleasant to breathe humid air.

So a recycling system on board the ISS collects humidity from the air, and water from urine and washing waste.

That water is treated in three ways to make it safe to drink:

1. The water is filtered to get rid of any particles.
2. The water is passed through chemicals to remove impurities.
3. Any bacteria and viruses that might be present are killed off.

But if water's so scarce, how do astronauts wash clothes? There's a simple answer.

Dwight Dirkswood, Space Log.
Earth date: 15 February

Got 'up' (ha ha). Buttermilk pancakes and tea made from recycled urine for breakfast. Day three of wearing that trusty old flight suit, so tossed it in the garbage. Quick rub down with a damp cloth and I'm shining like a rehydrated egg! On with the new outfit and I'm off for a bit of Earth-gazing.

That's right. Clothes aren't washed in space. They're simply worn for up to a week and then stored for later return to Earth.

This arrangement isn't perfect. After all, dirty washing takes up valuable space. But the Russians are working on a rather clever solution: underwear that can be eaten.

How do you think that might work?

(a) It gets so dirty it 'eats' itself.
(b) Lab rats can be trained to munch through dirty underwear.
(c) A bacterial cocktail just loves to digest them.

Answer: (c).

At the Institute for Biological and Medical Problems in Moscow, a team of brave scientists is working on a germ-based 'waste-degradation unit'.

Bugs living in these units will digest astronauts' cotton and paper underpants and produce methane gas as a result.

The best bit about this plan is that this methane gas could be used as fuel for a spacecraft. So, one day, you might go into space in a craft powered by dirty knickers!

The challenges of eating

Of course, when you change your clothes so rarely, you have to be a bit more careful with your food. Luckily, eating in space is one of the things you'll have trained for in the vomit comet. When there's a risk that chips could float up in front of your eyes, or spaghetti wrap itself round your head, you have to use a lot more care than you might at your dining table on Earth.

Laying the table

Psychologists know it's important to have contact with other people, so they made sure there was a dining table on the ISS. This way, astronauts can gather round and chat while they eat.

Magnets keep cutlery stuck to the table. Next to your knife, fork and spoon, you'll also put a pair of scissors. Without them, you'll find it tricky to cut open your food packets!

If you go for something liquid, like soup, you'll be sucking it out of a plastic bag with a straw. It won't be dainty. But no one wants globules of chicken soup floating away into the life-support systems.

But you will be able to eat more solid dishes with a knife and fork. Dishes with sauce are very popular — because they're likely to stay stuck together on your plate, and to your cutlery.

 ## Food time

In the early days of space travel, most food was dehydrated (the water was removed) to preserve it for the duration of the mission. Astronauts had to eat disgusting things like bite-size 'meal cubes' and freeze-dried powders.

Space food has come on quite a bit since then, but dehydration is still used. A soggy dish like macaroni cheese is dried out and put into packets. When you're ready to eat, you'll have to rehydrate it by spurting in some hot water to make it edible. Other meals can be packed into cans and the contents reheated in small food warmers.

There are other space food treatments. For example, meats are blasted with radioactivity to kill any bugs that might be inside. (Don't worry, it's quite safe — this is an accepted way to wipe out germs in food on Earth.)

But some foods don't need any 'treatment' at all. Coated chocolates, coated peanuts and chewing gum are all blasted up in their 'natural' form.

In fact, there's an astonishing choice of food in space. Your local restaurant would be very hard pressed to do better.

Here's a sample ISS menu.

MENU

- - - - - - - -

BREAKFAST

Fruit yoghurt
French toast
Apples, oranges
Buttermilk pancakes
Oatmeal
All served with coffee, tea, cocoa and juices

- - - - - - - -

LUNCH

Chicken teriyaki with spring vegetables
Beef enchilada with Spanish rice
Sautéed fish

- - - - - - - -

DINNER

Cream of broccoli soup
Wonton soup

Vegetable lasagne with tomato sauce
Baked ham with candied yams
Chicken pot pie

Chocolate cheesecake
Coconut cream pie
Chocolate fudge

Bill Brain's Top Tips: ———————————
Being in space dulls your sense of taste. Most astronauts get desperate for spicy foodstuffs like salsa and chilli sauce. If you're not keen on these, search around for something equally tastebud-blasting while you're still on Earth. You'll be able to pre-order it from space meal supplies — and it will travel with you to the ISS. ———————————

But what if you're itching for something that's just not on the menu? What if you're desperate for a take-away?

Well, it's not impossible. Even 400 kilometres from Earth.

 ### Pizza please!
In April 2001, Pizza Hut delivered the first pizza into space. It was carried on board a Russian Progress craft used to supply the ISS. The strange salami pizza got a thumbs-up from cosmonaut Yuri Usachov.

Why salami? Pepperoni is the usual ingredient but it has only a short shelf life. On the other hand, salami would stay edible during the trip to the ISS. The company also added extra salt and spices, to tickle Usachov's space-weary tongue.

This long-distance delivery broke another record — for the most expensive pizza ever. In fact, the stunt cost Pizza Hut about US$1 million. But it didn't cost lucky Usachov a cent! Or in his case, a rouble.

Pizza is now stocked on the ISS. So you can tuck into a slice of cheese, meat, vegetable or supreme pizza whenever you like. But you won't get a cola to go with it.

Bill Brain: Professor, why no cola in space?

KOSMOSKI: Well Coca-Cola did develop a can for use in space. The Coke was in a bag inside the can. There was compressed carbon-dioxide gas round the bag. This kept the drink fizzy. And in 1985, astronauts on the shuttle Challenger did drink Coke, but doctors were worried.

Brain: Why?

KOSMOSKI: They thought drinking a fizzy liquid could be harmful in micro G because it could be more difficult to burp. If you have a build-up of gas in your gut which you cannot belch out, it could be very unpleasant!

Brain: So, if not cola, then what?

KOSMOSKI: Well, you'll simply take a drink bag, attach it to a dispenser in the ISS 'kitchen', and fill it up with water or one of the wide range of still drinks on offer. Unless the Russians get their way ... Today, I have received a letter from my dear friends at the Russian Academy of Agricultural Science. My genius colleagues have come up with a truly wonderful invention: beer, designed specially for drinking in space! No alcohol, sadly. But, I hear, it contains added herbs and vitamins – with the aim of keeping up cosmonauts' health and spirits. I will drink to that!

So, it's been a long day. You've managed a shower. You've got most of your dinner into your mouth, rather than all over your flight suit. You're even an expert with the strange space toilet. It's time to sleep. Where do you do it?

 ## The challenges of sleeping

Most astronauts choose not to float free. They strap a pillow to their head and hook up their sleeping bag to the wall of the ISS.

But location is very important.

When you breathe out on Earth, that warm air tends to rise away from your face. This is a good thing, because your exhaled air contains a lot of carbon dioxide gas.

But warm air doesn't rise in space. This means there's a danger that exhaled carbon dioxide could pool round your head. This could starve your body of oxygen and leave you waking up gasping, with a terrible headache.

The solution is to choose a sleeping spot close to a ventilator fan to ensure a good supply of fresh air.

 Bill Brain's Top Tips: _____
You might also want to bring a pair of earplugs — the air filters, fans and other equipment will make for a noisy night's sleep. _____

On the ISS, you might go to sleep about 10 p.m. Greenwich Mean Time (the local time in London, as well as onboard the space station). They'll wake you at about six the next 'morning'.

That leaves you with a 16-hour day to fill. Washing and eating only takes so long, even when you're not used it. So what else do astronauts do?

- -

Dwight Dirkswood, Space Log.
Earth date: 18 February

6.00 a.m. Woke up. Unhooked sleeping bag. Saw station commander moving his mouth as though he was talking. But no words coming out. Thought I'd turned deaf, then remembered to take out the earplugs!
6.30 a.m. Fortified myself with coffee and sticky scrambled egg.
7.00 a.m. Kicked germ ass! Squirted anti-bug liquid on to a cloth and zapped the work areas.
7.30 a.m. Strapped myself into the treadmill for an hour and came out redder than those beet-roots I used to love to munch back in Star City.
8.30 a.m. Sent an email back home.
9.00 a.m. Checked on the seeds in the lab.
9.30 a.m. Prepared for an EVA...

- -

EVA stands for *Extravehicular Activity* – which means venturing outside your spacecraft.

That calls for some pretty special preparation. In the next chapter, you'll learn all about the kit that'll keep you alive out there in space.

CHAPTER 6

SPACE GEAR

'One of my favourite memories is hanging with
one hand on the Space Station, and swinging
out so I could look across Earth.'
Spacewalking American astronaut Jim Reilly

Going for a spacewalk

Want to follow in Jim's 'footsteps'? Then you'll need to
learn all about NASA's EMU – the Extravehicular Mobility
Unit – the big white suit you'll have to trust with your life.

Let's start by testing your knowledge of unprotected
life in space.

BILL BRAIN'S ASTRO QUIZ

1. If a person was accidentally blasted out through an ISS hatch, would they:

(a) explode?

(b) die, because their blood boils?

(c) freeze and burn to death in seconds?

Answer: both (b) and (c). In fact, you wouldn't explode in the vacuum of space. But the sudden drop in pressure would make your liquid blood start to convert into a gas — it would bubble and 'boil'. (Above 20,000 metres, humans need pressurized suits to stop fluids in their body boiling, and to provide enough oxygen to their lungs.)

The side of you facing away from the Sun would be exposed to -100°C, enough to freeze you solid in no time — but the side of you facing the Sun would be quickly roasted, at a temperature of 120°C. If you were very unlucky, you might also be blasted by a 'micrometeoroid' — a tiny space rock.

But luckily you wouldn't feel the pain for long. In seconds, you'd be unconscious due to the lack of oxygen.

To deal with these excruciating extremes, you need clothing to match. This doesn't come cheap — one EMU costs about US$12 million. But it does have to function as an independent mini-spacecraft. For at least seven hours, it will provide water, oxygen, pressure and jetpack propulsion, and stop you losing too much heat. In itself, it's a spectacular feat of space engineering.

EMU – EXTRAVEHICULAR MOBILITY UNIT

WEIGHT: 118 kilograms on Earth
NUMBER OF LAYERS: 12
MATERIALS: include fibreglass, nylon, Kevlar (bullet-proof)

LIQUID COOLING AND VENTILATION GARMENT

A one-piece, mesh, inner suit that goes on first. It is fitted with tubes that carry cool water. This water carries heat away from the astronaut's body and prevents it overheating.

HARD UPPER TORSO (HUT)

A hard, vest-shaped, fibreglass shell supporting the arms, upper body, life-support backpack, helmet and control module.

LOWER TORSO ASSEMBLY

This one-piece outer unit covers the lower body and is attached to the HUT.

EXTRAVEHICULAR VISOR ASSEMBLY (EVA)

This fits over an inner helmet, which is made from tough see-through plastic. The visor is coloured gold to filter sunlight and stop you being blinded. It is also designed to stop the astronaut losing too much heat, and to give some protection in case a tiny space rock hurtles in his or her direction. The EVA is also fitted with four lights and a TV camera.

PRIMARY LIFE-SUPPORT SUBSYSTEM (PLSS)

The upper part of the backpack that contains oxygen tanks, carbon-dioxide filters, electrical power, cooling water and radio-communication equipment. Oxygen flows in above the astronaut's head and is sucked out around their lower legs and feet.

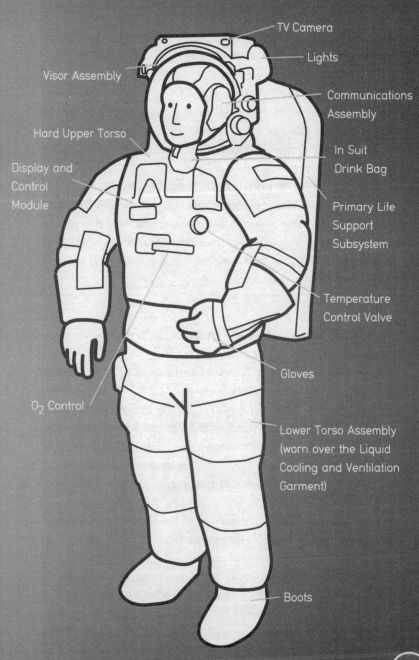

TV Camera

Lights

Visor Assembly

Communications
Assembly

Hard Upper Torso

In Suit
Drink Bag

Display and
Control
Module

Primary Life
Support
Subsystem

Temperature
Control Valve

Gloves

O₂ Control

Lower Torso Assembly
(worn over the Liquid
Cooling and Ventilation
Garment)

Boots

Below the PLSS is a Secondary Oxygen Pack, which can provide an emergency supply of 30 minutes of oxygen.

DISPLAY AND CONTROL MODULE
This unit is mounted on the chest. It can make it difficult to see, so there is a mirror attached to the sleeve. The module contains all the switches needed to operate and monitor the PLSS.

SERVICING AND COOLING UMBILICAL
Sometimes you'll see spacewalkers attached to their craft by a long line. This is called the Servicing and Cooling Umbilical. It's used to provide electricity, oxygen, water and communication lines while the spacewalker is still close to 'home'. This helps conserve the supplies built into the EMU.

The basic space shuttle EMU was modified slightly for use on the International Space Station. The new suit can be adjusted to fit different-sized astronauts and can easily be cleaned on board the station. It also contains mini-heaters, like fingertip heaters in the glove. This is because spacewalks from the ISS are much frostier than a walk from the shuttle. The shuttle pilot can manoeuvre the craft so that a space-walker regularly faces the Sun – and doesn't get too cold. But the ISS can't be moved in this way.

Intrepid TV reporter Bill Brain went to Professor Kosmoski's garage to try out a suit. Here's his report:

Bill Brain: Folks, I'm back with space boffin Professor Karl Kosmoski. As you can see, I'm talking to you from an EMU. That's the suit, you

understand. The emu might be one of the world's fastest, most elegant running birds. But this EMU is nothing like its namesake! Ha ha! Professor, this is the most unwieldy thing I've ever had the displeasure of walking in.

KOSMOSKI: Indeed. It's like moving around in a football pumped full of air.

Brain: It helps that there are these movable sections built in at the knees, elbows and other joints to help me walk, but hey, I wouldn't swap my shorts for this outfit ... ever!

KOSMOSKI: You would in space.

Brain: Well, yes.

KOSMOSKI: Because in your shorts, you would freeze and boil at the same time.

No astronaut will tell you that taking a spacewalk is like strolling down the high street on a Saturday afternoon. You will, of course, train long and hard in an EMU in the giant swimming pools at Star City or the Johnson Space Center. But you won't learn to move fast. You'll go slowly. You'll get hot. Your muscles will ache. And what if you want to go to the toilet? Or eat? Or sneeze?

What do you think? Turn to the quiz on the next page.

BILL BRAIN'S ASTRO QUIZ

On a spacewalk...

1. If you get hungry, you must:
(a) wait until the walk is finished? .
(b) nibble on a space bar?
(c) choose from a selection of in-suit snacks?

2. If you need to sneeze, you must:
(a) turn your head to one side?
(b) quickly pull a tissue from the in-helmet pouch?
(c) swallow it?

3. If you want to go to the toilet, you must:
(a) do everything into a big nappy?
(b) go back to the spacecraft to use the toilet facilities?
(c) switch on the in-suit waste-collection system?

Answers

1. *(b)* Inside the inner helmet is a slot to hold a fruit-and-cereal bar to snack on if you get hungry during your walk. As you take a bite, the bar moves up in the slot. But you must be careful to eat it quickly and cleanly — having crumbs floating around in your helmet would be pretty unpleasant. There's also a straw in your helmet that is connected to a plastic water pouch inside the Hard Upper Torso. This pouch can hold up to 1.9 litres of water.

2. *(a)* If you must sneeze, this is your only real option. Whatever you do, you must be careful not to sneeze all over your visor — it could make seeing out very tricky.

3. *(a)* Yes, a nappy. Both male and female astronauts wear big absorbable garments to gather their waste! They are effective — collecting about one litre of fluid without letting any dribble out — but they're not the most glamorous of space wear!

In fact, it takes only about five minutes to get out of an EMU — but it's the getting in that takes the real time. Before going on a spacewalk, there's a long preparation procedure.

Here's what you'll do:

1. *Pedal away on an exercise bike while breathing pure oxygen.* This helps get your body ready for the oxygen-only breathing supply in the EMU. It also helps remove nitrogen from your blood. This is essential because as pressure drops, as it does when you're in an EMU, nitrogen dissolved in your blood can form gas bubbles. (Divers know this as the 'bends'.) These bubbles can kill.

2. *Slowly lower your surrounding pressure to match the lower pressure inside the EMU.* If you'll be working out of the space shuttle, everyone inside also experiences the drop in pressure. If you'll be spacewalking from the ISS, you'll go into an isolated airlock, and let the pressure fall.

3. *Put on your EMU.* First you step into the Lower Torso Assembly (once you've got your inner cooling suit on, of course). Then you'll breathe in pure oxygen for about an hour. Pure oxygen is used because if you breathed normal air at lower than Earth pressure, you would get dangerously little oxygen into your lungs — the same reason climbers high up on Mount Everest carry oxygen cylinders with them.

4. *Step out into space ...*

The person who stepped out for the very first time must have been incredibly brave. Who was he?

BILL BRAIN'S HALL OF ASTRO FAME NO.6

Alexei Arkhipovich Leonov
· *The first ever spacewalker*

Born: 1934, Russia

A highly talented artist, Leonov joined the military and trained to fly fighter jets. In 1965, Leonov let himself out of his Voskhod capsule, 177 kilometres above Earth. Attached by a cord, he spent more than 10 minutes taking pictures and practising moving about. Afterwards, Leonov was picked as the commander of the first Soviet mission to the Moon. But when NASA's Apollo 11 beat them to it in 1969, the mission was cancelled. Leonov continued as a cosmonaut, and continued painting — especially pictures of what he saw in space. Of course, Leonov's spacesuit was less complex by comparison with today's EMUs. The Russians now use a suit similar to the EMU, called the Orlan.

Like the EMUs, ways of getting about while wearing them have become a lot more complicated since Leonov's day.

SAFER travel

Ever dreamed of zipping around with a jet-powered back-pack? With the SAFER you can. SAFER stands for Simplified Aid for Extravehicular Rescue. It's designed to get a drifting astronaut back to safety using jets of nitrogen gas. Inbuilt controls, similar to those used for computer games, will let you fly up and down and side to side with precision. But, in truth, 'zipping' is a bit of an exaggeration ... The fastest you'll go with SAFER is three metres per second – about the same as a slow jog.

Choose your outfit

Of course, astronauts aren't always kitted out in bulky EMUs. For take-off, re-entry and day-to-day life in space, they wear different outfits.

Launch and return

You'll wear what's called an Advanced Crew Escape Suit (ACES). This bright orange suit can be fully pressurized –

in case you have to bail out at high altitude in an emergency. On your back, you'll wear a parachute pack that also contains a life raft and emergency drinking water. And when you're returning to Earth, you'll also wear an anti-gravity suit underneath your ACES. This anti-gravity suit squeezes your legs to help prevent blood pooling in them (see page 30).

Day to day

Got a favourite piece of clothing you wish you could wear every single day? You'll have to leave it behind when you go into space. Before your mission, you'll get to choose from a special range of clothing. This includes all-in-one flight suits, jackets, shirts, underwear and sleep shorts. All of your kit is made from flame-retardant material and is fitted with sealable pockets, to hold pens, scissors, tools and so on.

Hand luggage

NASA and Star City provide all your clothing and kit. But astronauts and cosmonauts are allowed to take up some personal belongings. And bring them back ...

Return of the Aliens

Scattered over Planet Earth are green organisms from space! There are more than twice as many as there are astronauts on Earth! And no one knows where they are ...

No fiction — this is true.

Every NASA Moon astronaut was allowed to take a few personal items along for the ride. In 1971, Jack Roosa took five different types of seeds into space with him. These seeds circled the Moon 34 times.

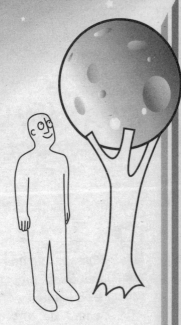

Back on Earth, these seeds were planted and grew into seedlings. And these seedlings became Moon Trees.

Everyone wanted a Moon Tree. NASA sent them to the White House, around the USA, and all over the world. Even the Emperor of Japan got one. But no one kept proper records of exactly where all the trees ended up. One NASA scientist has managed to track down 40 of them, but he's still looking for more.

Roosa's choice was unusual, but certainly not the strangest of all. Astronaut Al Shepard picked golf balls to fly with him. John Young took a corned-beef sandwich. You'll get your own choice to make when your mission is ready.

But whatever you take with you, it will have to be thoroughly checked. NASA's 'master sniffer' himself might give your objects the once over. Master sniffer? Again — no fiction. To get wind of the truth, you'll have to read on ...

CHAPTER 7

SPACE HEADACHES

Every astronaut must be ready to deal with anything (no coincidence maybe that most NASA astronauts were Scouts or Guides as kids). These could be anything from little things that might seem silly on Earth, to full-blown disasters. In the next two chapters, you'll learn what you might have to contend with, and how to cope with them.

Awful odours

Of all the possible dangers in space, you might think that nasty niffs would be far down the list. But did you know that bad smells once caused a mission to be cancelled?

The details are sketchy. However in 1976, Russian cosmonauts were forced to make an emergency landing when an 'acrid odour' became unbearable!

One man 'nose' all about this kind of trouble – NASA's 'master sniffer'. He leads a team of 25 people dedicated to sniffing out every item that flies on the shuttle. They test everything: from paints, fabrics, shoes and shaving cream to the Chuckie Bear toy one astronaut was determined to take into orbit.

BILL BRAIN'S ASTRO QUIZ

Why do you think smells could be more of a problem in space than on Earth:

(a) Astronauts' noses become more sensitive in space?

(b) The confined quarters of a spacecraft means there's nowhere for odours to escape?

(c) Astronauts have such critical duties to perform that they can't be distracted by the scent of perfumed socks or nicely warmed Velcro?

Answer: (b). The limited space and the heat are the real problem. Imagine driving inside a new car with the windows down. The smell would hardly bother you. Now imagine sitting in that same car with the windows wound up on a hot day. The heat would speed the evaporation of stinky chemicals from the plastics and fabrics. And there'd be nowhere for those smells to escape.

NASA has to make sure that nothing too smelly makes it up into space. 'Electronic noses' do exist, but the agency swears by the real human thing.

Say you want to take this book with you into space. Here's how it would get tested:

1. The book is loaded into a sealed container and heated to 49°C for 72 hours.

2. Gases given off by the hot book are injected into two pieces of equipment, designed to identify the different components of that gas and their amounts.

3. If none of those gases is toxic, the book will pass on to five people on the 'Odor Panel'.

4. These people smell it and grade it on a scale from 0 (for undetectable) to 4 (for very irritating or revolting).

5. The average of these scores is calculated. If it's higher than 2.4, this book will get rejected.

Of course, some space stinks can't be prevented. If you fart in your spacecraft, you'd better start apologizing fast. On a more practical level, you could try using those earplugs to block up your nose! Because it will take a lot longer for the smell to disappear than it would on Earth. (One reason, perhaps, why you won't find beans and more beans on the average space-shuttle menu.)

Think you might fancy retiring to the Odor Panel once your astronaut days are over? The recruitment procedure is strict. No one with any allergies or breathing problems can become a NASA sniffer, because their noses are already irritated by things like cat hairs or household dust. Then you'll have to pass the **'10-bottle test'**.

You can try a version of this test at home. Here's how:

YOU'LL NEED:
- 10 glass jars with lids
- 7 slightly smelly everyday items, like washing-up liquid and elastic bands

WHAT TO DO:

1. Make sure the jars are thoroughly washed out and aired.

2. Put each of the seven items in a jar and close the lids. (Three jars remain empty.)

3. Ask someone to blindfold you and then mix up the jars.

4. Sniff all the jars. Identify the empty ones.

To make it harder, ask someone to set up the test without you watching, so you don't know what you're supposed to be sniffing.

Members of NASA's Odor Panel check their noses every three months using the 10-bottle test.

Stressed stomachs

There's not a lot that trainee astronauts can do to get their noses ready for life in space, but they can try to prepare their stomachs for the trip. So, how about a nice supper of yoghurt made from bacteria from cosmonauts' guts? Why? Because space flight is likely to make you stressed – and stress can weaken your immune system. This complex system of cells and chemicals helps you to fight infections and keeps you healthy. If your immune system is in poor shape, you'll be in the same state.

Bill Brain: Let the Professor explain this.

KOSMOSKI: Inside you right now are millions of bacteria. They're lurking in your stomach, your intestines, your bowels, even your mouth! This is quite normal. Some of these bacteria are completely harmless. But others could make you sick if they grew in too many numbers.

If your immune system is working properly, it will keep levels of 'bad' bacteria in check – keeping you healthy. But if it is weakened for some reason, it might struggle to do this job properly – and you could fall sick.

One way to help your immune system is to keep high levels of the harmless bacteria in your body. How could you do this? Well, you might harvest them from the guts of a healthy person!

Who's the healthiest person you can think of? An athlete? The Russian Space Agency were looking for people in peak fitness, whose training, diet and health were closely monitored by legions of doctors. And where do you find them? Yes, the Russians reasoned that taking good bacteria from the mouth and guts of cosmonauts would be perfect!

As one Russian scientist said, 'We only collect cultures that are able to withstand extreme conditions!'

The Agency then made yoghurt using these bacteria, for other cosmonauts to eat on long missions in space.

But what do other scientists think?

The answer is that they're not desperately impressed by the Russians' argument. They say there's nothing wrong with it, but they doubt that bacteria from a cosmonaut would be any better than the average person's.

System boost

In fact, scientists have investigated all kinds of ways of boosting your immune system.

BILL BRAIN'S ASTRO QUIZ

Which of these do you think might work:

(a) Drinking a tonic made from Chinese ants?
(b) Snacking on blue-green algae?
(c) Eating a bar of chocolate?

In Tibet, the Chinese ant *Polyrhachis vicina* is made into an immune-boosting drink. British scientists who studied the insect found that it contains a lot of zinc — a metal known to pep up the immune system.

Experiments on a blue-green algae called *Spirulina* have shown that it can triple levels of certain immune-system chemicals.

And chocolate seems to work simply because people enjoy it. Even the smell of chocolate can improve your immune activity. Be careful not to eat too much, though — astronauts can't be fat!

Housekeeping

Of course, one essential for tip-top health is to keep as clean as possible. Not only your body (and as you know from Chapter Five, that's not easy in space), but your surroundings. Yes, in space, you're going to have to get out the vacuum-cleaner.

Dirt sucks

Many pieces of equipment have in-built fans to cool them down. On the space shuttle, astronauts use a mini-vacuum-cleaner or pieces of sticky tape to clean the fans' screens. If they didn't, bits of hair and dust could clog them up, making the equipment overheat. This has happened — TV monitors in the shuttle have shut down because their fans weren't cleaned properly.

Lost property

Astronauts aren't always perfect at keeping a close check of their belongings. The people who have to give the shuttle a thorough cleaning after each mission have found a whole range of objects, including a pen, coins and a contact lens! Once, they even found a dead tree frog – but they think the frog must have hopped on board after the shuttle landed!

Muck and mould

If they could, tiny life forms would take over the shuttle, the Soyuz and the International Space Station. Minute bacteria, viruses, moulds and fungi are carried up by astronauts. No matter how clean you are, you still have millions of bacteria all over your skin, in your hair, your mouth, even your eyes.

GERM FILES –
URGENT READING FOR ALL ASTRONAUTS!

BACTERIA
RISK FACTOR: Low

Bacteria grow faster in space. Some types of bacteria that produce antibiotics (which is used in medicine) reproduce three times faster in microgravity. No one is exactly sure why. But bacteria are surrounded by a fluid. They swim in it and get nutrients from it. It's possible that this fluid mixes differently in micro G, and gives bacteria more food to eat!

MOULDS
RISK FACTOR: High

Moulds love damp surroundings. They thrive in humid, hot environments, such as the ISS. If left unchecked, they could munch their way through vital components, putting astronauts' lives at risk, as happened on Russia's old space station, Mir. In 2000, cosmonauts reported the windows getting foggy. The culprit – a mass of mould obscuring the glass! (Mould doesn't eat metal or glass. It feeds on organic matter, such as flakes of dead skin and other human cast-offs. It then produces acids that can corrode steel, glass and plastic.)

MUTANT MOULDS AND FUNGI
RISK FACTOR: Extreme danger

When Mir was finally ditched in 2001, moulds had been living in isolation on it for 15 years. Some scientists were afraid they might have evolved into terrible super-powerful species, and that when returning Mir fragments hit Earth, the moulds and fungi could spread ...

'The mutant fungi do exist and in future could do serious damage to humanity,' said one Russian space expert. They haven't yet been found!

To help keep moulds in check, you and your fellow shuttle or ISS crewmates will have to get out germ-killing liquid and regularly wipe every surface in sight.

If bug-infested nightmares don't disturb your sleep, there are other things that will. Any would-be astronaut has to know why.

From: Dwight Dirkswood
Date: Mon March 2nd, 02:02
To: Jean and Chuck Dirkswood
Subject: Private

Hi Mom and Dad,

It's about 2 a.m. your time and I'm wide awake. That's because it's dawn. Again. On the space station here, I see 15 of these dawns every 24 hours. It's always morning — and I'm always yawning! I'm finding it pretty tricky to get a good stretch of sleep, like you always recommended, Mom. In fact, I feel like I've got jet lag. Permanently. Not even a nice bedtime snack seems to help.

Your seriously sleepy son,

Dwight

The problem is: your body is tuned to life on Earth. Your brain responds to changes in light, and to the hour of the day. After 90 days in space, your body clock – that part of your brain that controls how awake, alert or sleepy you feel – begins to lose track of time. The amount of time you spend asleep, and the quality of that sleep, drops. This can be dangerous, for two reasons:

1. Scientists know that people make more mistakes when they're very tired.
2. You could drop off at any time.

One American cosmonaut who spent time on Russia's Mir station said he tried to be strict about his sleeping hours. But his two colleagues weren't so careful. 'They'd nod off and float right past you!' he said.

Space scientists know that if people are to spend really long periods on a craft, travelling to Mars or further, they're going to have to discover ways of tricking body clocks into thinking they're still on Earth.

In the meantime, many astronauts take pills to help them get a decent 'night's' sleep. But which of the following do you think could also be worth a try:

1. Drinking a cup of warm milk?
2. A brisk treadmill run to tire you out?
3. Counting sheep?

Answers:
1. Yes. Milk contains a natural chemical that helps people go to sleep.

2. No. Exercise makes your body feel awake. Sleep scientists say you shouldn't exercise within about two hours of trying to sleep.

3. No. It's just too boring. You'll need to encourage your mind to lose focus on the day's exciting activities. To do that, you'll have to picture a more interesting though relaxing scene, like being on holiday. Imagine it now: going for a walk along the beach, floating on the sea ...

If lack of sleep is a danger, there is something worse. And it's invisible ...

Space rays

They'll be all around you, firing at your craft with a terrible speed! Not from the gun of an unfriendly alien, but from galaxies outside the solar system – and from our very own Sun.

The Sun belches out bursts of 'radioactive' particles into space. Every eleven years this activity reaches a peak, with massive solar flares (huge eruptions of matter from the Sun). Earth has its very own 'deflector shield' – a magnetic shield round the planet which absorbs radiation from space. Together with the atmosphere, it keeps the worst of these rays from zapping you and your family. But in space, you'll lose this shield.

So what can astronauts do to protect themselves?

1. The walls of a spacecraft must be thick enough to stop most of the rays coming through.
2. Astronauts should spend as little time as possible on spacewalks outside the craft, especially when scientists know the Sun is bursting with more energy than usual!

Cosmic rays, dodgy stomachs and poor sleep are just three of the potential problems you'll encounter. Are you ready to move on to the really scary scenarios? Then take a deep breath ...

CHAPTER 8

READY FOR ANYTHING

Now for the scary stuff. The real dangers. The kind of cosmic catastrophes that could make even the toughest would-be astronaut wobble like a rehydrated jelly.

Let's start with ...

Fire

DISASTER FILE: ENTRY 1

CHALLENGER SPACE SHUTTLE

1986: The shuttle Challenger took off safely with seven people on board. But seals between parts of the Solid Rocket Boosters failed, allowing gases to leak. Fifty-nine seconds after launch, a flame formed and spread, and the shuttle exploded.

MIR SPACE STATION

1997: A fire on Russia's Mir filled the living and working quarters with smoke. The fire started when one of the cosmonauts was working with a defective canister of a flammable chemical. Burning this chemical produced oxygen for the cosmonauts on board. But in this instance, the fire escaped. The cosmonauts quickly grabbed foam-spurting extinguishers and managed to put out the flames. But they had to wear filter masks and use oxygen packs until Mir's climate-control systems cleared the air.

These disasters indicate that space travel is a risky business. NASA recently worked out that one in every 428 shuttle launches will result in disaster. But Disaster File: Entry 2 shows that if the fire isn't too large and if you have access to it, it doesn't have to be deadly – even in space.

To be an astronaut, you have to believe that the bonuses outweigh those potential risks. Remember first space tourist Dennis Tito describing his mission as 'paradise'.

Accident

What if one of those Mir cosmonauts had been badly burned? What if you suddenly fell seriously ill during your stay on the ISS? The nearest ambulance is 400 kilometres away. Which means you'll need ... *Space ER*.

ASTRONAUT *(missing two fingers)*: It's terrible, commander. The pain. The blood. You have to help me!

COMMANDER: Stiff upper lip, astronaut! Remember, two of the crew members on each shuttle mission are also designated Crew Medical Officers.

ASTRONAUT: But one of those is me. And the other ...

COMMANDER: Ah, yes, is me! So, wait two ticks and I'll fetch the Shuttle-Orbiter Medical System.

ASTRONAUT *(relief)*: At last, commander. I'm saved!

Bill Brain's Notes:

Crew Medical Officers get extra training on how to use the Shuttle-Orbiter Medical System. But they're often not real doctors, and the Shuttle-Orbiter Medical System is not as fancy as it sounds!

In fact, the Shuttle-Orbiter Medical System consists of two medical kits:

MEDICATIONS AND BANDAGE KIT

This contains:

- *Pills, such as aspirins and anti-diarrhoea tablets*
- *Bandages for covering wounds or keeping broken limbs still*
- *Lotions and creams for cuts and rashes*

EMERGENCY MEDICAL KIT

This contains:

- *Medicines to be given by injection, such as adrenaline solution to kick-start a stopped heart.*

- *Equipment for performing minor surgery — a scalpel and needles for stitches*
- *Instruments to inspect the body — like heart rate and blood-pressure monitors*
- *Tests for different types of bacterial infection.*

Back at Mission Control, experts can keep a continuous watch on conditions in the shuttle or ISS. They monitor cabin pressure, oxygen content, temperature, humidity and radiation levels – and can spot changes that could make you sick. If you're involved in a particularly dangerous operation, like performing a spacewalk, sensors attached to your chest will tell them how your heart's performing. These kind of sensors can also provide doctors on the ground with vital information if an astronaut becomes unwell.

So far, there have been no reports of any cosmonaut or astronaut falling dangerously ill in space. But if you did become very sick on a shuttle or even the ISS, you could be back on Earth in a matter of hours.

Astro-surgery
NASA knows that on long missions, to Mars, for example, a speedy return to Earth would not be possible. So it's working with an international agency of surgeons to develop a virtual-reality operating theatre. This gory virtual-reality system will let astronauts practise fixing broken legs and arms.

'Dead Guy Test'
Trainee astronauts also have to practise rescuing stricken spacewalkers. Real-life disaster drills on the International Space Station have shown it's best to attach your tether to your unconscious partner and tug on the cord to pull both of

you safely back to the airlock.

Again, there have been no reports of spacewalkers passing out and needing rescuing. But they have got into other difficulties.

Bill Brain: Professor Kosmoski has a real-life story for you, my readers.

KOSMOSKI: Yes, indeed: the case of Robert Curbeam, American astronaut and true space survivor!

Curbeam flew on the space shuttle Atlantis. He was conducting a spacewalk at the time that the Destiny laboratory was being attached to the Unity module of the International Space Station. Pipes carrying ammonia ran between these two modules. On Earth, ammonia is an unpleasant gas, which can kill in high enough quantities. On the ISS, it is used as a coolant to carry heat from electronics in the laboratory.

When Curbeam was partway through his walk, one of the pipes sprang a leak, and ammonia spurted every-where. It quickly became a cloud of frozen crystals enveloping poor Curbeam. The EMU protected him from harm, but the crystals on his suit could have posed a danger to the astronauts inside Atlantis – once inside, the crystals might have reverted to a dangerous gas.

Quickly, Curbeam's fellow spacewalker produced a large brush to dust down his friend's suit.

Next, Curbeam stayed longer than he should have in the burning rays of the Sun so that its heat would get rid of any crystals missed by the brush. Then, Curbeam and his colleague sat in the airlock while it was pressurized, depressurized and pressurized again. This meant that any crystals remaining would evaporate in the airlock, not in the shuttle.

The result: Curbeam and his colleague made it safely back into the shuttle, and there wasn't a weepy, ammonia-affected eye in sight.

Of course spurting pipes, accidental fires or sudden sicknesses aren't your only possible space emergencies. There's another: *Impact*.

DISASTER FILE: ENTRY 3

SPACE SHUTTLE COLUMBIA

2003: During launch, a piece of foam fell from a fuel tank and crashed onto heat-resistant tiles on Columbia's wing. This impact damaged the tiles, and when Columbia re-entered the Earth's atmosphere on 1 February, super-hot gases entered the wing. These gases melted the aluminium frame and caused the shuttle to disintegrate, killing everyone on board.

This tragedy was caused by a part of the shuttle's own fuel tank breaking away and smashing into the orbiter. But there are other objects out there that could threaten a crew. In fact, there are literally thousands of them, screaming in orbit, with the power to obliterate your flimsy craft.

And the worst part? We put them there.

Space objects !

See if you can pick the one object that has never been spotted whizzing in orbit round Earth:

1. *A glove?*
2. *Specks of paint?*
3. *A bashed-up Moon rocket?*
4. *A garbage bag?*
5. *A skunk?*
6. *A dog?*

Answers:

1. During the first US spacewalk in 1965, astronaut Edward White lost a glove. It probably stayed in orbit round Earth for one month before burning up while re-entering our atmosphere.
2. Thousands of specks of paint from broken-up satellites and damaged spacecraft are whizzing round Earth at ferocious speeds.
3. In 2002, scientists spotted what at first they thought could be a new Moon. In fact, it turned out to be an old American Apollo rocket.
4. Russia's Mir space station — which was taken out of service in March 2001 — space-dumped hundreds of garbage bags, along with other unwanted objects.

5. If you said a skunk, you're right! Skunks would be far too smelly to blast into space!

6. In 1957, the Russian Space Agency launched a dog called Laika *(which is Russian for 'barker')*. Laika underwent training to prepare her for the noise and terrible vibrations of take-off. Her capsule was fitted with an automatic food dispenser. But according to sensors that measured her heart rate, she suffered extreme stress after launch, and died from overheating within a few hours.

There are thousands of chucked-away, man-made objects in space – and many could pose a terrible threat.

Think a speck of paint isn't scary? Well, a speck from a satellite once splatted into a space-shuttle window and gouged out a pit half a centimetre wide. If it had been the size of a cricket ball, it could have wiped out that mission.

The shuttles and Soyuz craft and the International Space Station are designed to withstand impacts from these man-made objects, and from other small chunks of space rock or meteorites.

DID YOU KNOW?
'Micro-meteoroid Orbital Debris' shielding is fitted to parts of the ISS. This shielding consists of a sheet of aluminium, 1.27 millimetres thick, separated from the module by a 10-centimetre gap. The aim: debris hitting the aluminium shield is broken up into a cloud, which softens its impact on the ISS.

But what if a big piece of junk was heading right for the ISS?

Answer: You'd need to take evasive action. Remember that the station has booster rockets, which you could use to manoeuvre out of the way of a rampaging garbage bag.

But how would you know it was coming? Who could give you warning?

Welcome to the 21st Space Wing ...

TRAINING FILE

THE 21ST SPACE WING

HEADQUARTERS: Peterson Air Force Base, Colorado, USA
MEMBERS: In 5 countries, crossing 9 time zones, with 43 units at 20 locations.
PRIMARY OBJECTIVES: To provide early warning of long-range missile attacks and foreign space launches, partly by manning the Space Surveillance Network.

Bill Brain: Professor, what is the Space Surveillance Network?

KOSMOSKI: This network has been tracking space objects since 1957. That was when the Russians launched the first ever craft to make it into space, Sputnik 1.

Using a network of 21 sensors on the ground and one

117

in space, it tracks all debris bigger than 10 centimetres across – that's more than 8,000 objects.

Data from these sensors are sent straight to the 1st Space Control Center at the Cheyenne Mountain Operations Center. If any chunk of space junk looks set to come within safety 'boxes' measuring 10 by 40 by 40 kilometres around the shuttle or ISS, the Center will send an alert straight to NASA. Job done!

NASA also has its own space junk monitoring system. It uses telescopes to monitor about 100,000 mini-fragments between 1 and 10 centimetres across.

Luckily, most space debris is orbiting at about twice as far away from Earth as the ISS and shuttle, and the chance of a collision with a big piece is very small.

Of course, very small isn't quite the same as non-existent. If the worst happened – and the ISS was struck and terribly damaged – or fire swept through faster than you and your fellow astronauts could fight it, it would be time to evacuate.

Evacuate!

Every trainee star sailor receives full instruction in ISS evacuation procedures. You'll also have regular drills in 'emergency descent'. Think of a fire-alarm drill at your school. You'll be told to be calm, no panicking, no shouting. It's the same in space. But instead of heading for a playing field, every ISS occupant will go to either the Soyuz TMA escape capsule or their own docked craft.

There are plans for a second escape capsule. But until that craft is ready, the number of people on the ISS is limited to the three who could escape in the TMA, plus any visitors who came – and could leave – in their own spacecraft.

DISASTER FILE: ENTRY 4

MIR SPACE STATION

No space station has ever been evacuated yet. But Mir came very close. In June 1997, an approaching cargo ship smashed into the side of the Progress station. One of the six modules was badly damaged, and Mir lost half its power. Michael Foale, an English astronaut on board, says the crew was minutes from bailing out. But they worked hard and got what could have been a terrible space disaster under control.

Of course, astronauts just aren't the types to be frozen by fear. If they were, they'd have been struck off the application list at the psychological screening.

But that doesn't mean astronauts are psychologically perfect. Mission Control knows that if it's to get the best out of you, it has to use some clever mind-manipulation of its own.

Turn to the next chapter to find out how ...

CHAPTER 9
MIND GAMES

Being an astronaut is astronomically hard work — so imagine being that astronaut's psychologist. You've selected someone you're pretty sure won't go crazy in space, but you have to make sure they stay happy, focused and fearless day after day after day.

For short missions lasting up to a couple of months, space is such a blast that this isn't too difficult. But even then, psychologists on the ground have a couple of tricks up their white-coated sleeves ...

Bill Brain: Professor, how does Mission Control stop astronauts from going nuts?

KOSMOSKI: Astronauts are a simple bunch. Floating about, playing games with their food. Kicking socks through the air like fantasy footballs. Children! Detect a little dose of depression and Mission Control hits them with ... music and family!

Music has an incredible effect on how you feel. If you don't like Russian pop music, you may feel like kicking someone who plays it all day. If you love it, you'll be bouncing around your space 'bedroom'.

Mission Control knows how important music is. It might wake you up with an energetic song it thinks is sure to get you out of that space sleeping bag and straight to the lab. Or, if you're on a longer mission, perhaps as a crew member on the ISS, it will send regular supplies of new CDs.

Psychologists have long been interested in the effects of music on the mind.

DID YOU KNOW?

Music can make people temporarily depressed. Mission Control would be well advised to stay away from psychologists' first choice for this effect: the desperately down beat *Russia Beneath the Yoke of the Mongols*, written by classical composer Prokofiev.

Warning: *don't try it out at home. You might not have the energy to get up and turn off the stereo!*

Music can even affect what you choose to buy in the supermarket. In one experiment, a psychologist found that when French music was playing, people bought much more French wine than usual. The same was true for German music and German wine. So if you feel like burgers for tea, why not try blasting your mum with American rock?

Warning: *first make sure she doesn't hate it, or you could be left with no tea at all.*

As well as music, Mission Control has a second secret psychological weapon: the family.

Regular contact with family back on Earth seems to be vital for keeping astronauts in good spirits. So all astronauts are allowed to have regular conversations with people at home. If your family can make it into Mission Control, you'll be able to have video chats; otherwise there's always your local ham radio operator.

DID YOU KNOW?

The first amateur radio in space blasted off in 1983 aboard a space shuttle. Using the handset on the shuttle, astronauts can talk to anyone with a handset receiver on Earth. This includes schoolchildren as well as family or friends.

Psychologists made sure an amateur radio was going to the ISS. International teams worked on perfecting a system to fit in to the Zvezda living module.

Talking to people on Earth seems to help astronauts in two ways:

1. Their family and friends give them morale-boosting support.
2. It's good to hear other voices and see other faces.

But being cooped up with a few other astronauts for a ten-day supply trip to the ISS is one thing. Can you think of five or so other people you'd willingly be trapped with on a mission lasting months – or even years?

Russian scientists have sifted through years of astro-data to identify three key periods in a typical star sailor's experience.

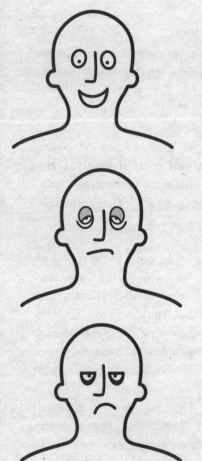

1. Phase One: general excitement at new surroundings, usually lasting around two months.

2. Phase Two: increasing tiredness and depression.

3. Phase Three: after about three months, irritability and deep depression.

The prospect of supporting a journey to Mars has some space psychologists rushing for their own couches. Just imagine what might happen ...

Dwight Dirkswood, Space Log.
Mars Mission 2030

Earth date: 30 January 2030
Blast off for our mission to Mars! Six months there, a couple of rosy months on the Red Planet, and six months back! It'll be a breeze!

Earth date: 28 February 2030
Everything tip-top. Spent the past couple of hours doing somersaults with my new best friends: Clare from England and New Zealand astronaut Jono. Starting to get through those peanut-chocs though.

Earth date: 27 April 2030
Two months to go before we get to Mars and things aren't going quite so well. This morning, Clare scoffed the last of the peanut-chocs. She knew they're my favourite. Then, Jono started saying some old Kiwi bloke was the first up Mount Everest, and I just know he wasn't!

Earth date: 15 May 2030
This is it. The full stop. The big enchilada. Hard to recall those happy first days. Now the tension. The arguing. The way Clare scratches her neck. That skanky metal music Jono won't stop playing. Darn it, it's over. I can't take it anymore. I'm out of here. Fire up the craft. I'm going home!

Psychologists have a good idea of the risks. In a recent experiment, trainee cosmonauts were locked into spacecraft simulators for months. Psychologists kept a close eye to see how they'd react.

The answer? Not well. Two of the men soon got into a fight.

Space psychologists have also studied other groups that spend months and months together to get a better idea of what goes wrong. Favourites for research are:

1. Scientists that spend the winter in Antarctica — once they're in, the severe weather means there can be no way out for months. There have been no reports of deadly encounters, but there have been fights.
2. Submariners. They have to spend weeks or months cramped up with the same old faces in uncomfortable conditions. But at least submarine sailors can have hundreds of other people to talk to.

But space mind-experts don't have to rely only on experiments or groups of non-astronauts. Before it was ditched in 2001, cosmonauts spent a combined total of almost 90,000 hours on the Russian Mir space station. A few brave pioneers spent well over a year in their confined quarters. Before Mir, the Russians had run smaller space stations, such as Salyut 7, and NASA had its own 'permanent' laboratory in space, called Skylab. There are no reports of cosmonauts coming to blows. But some certainly did suffer.

Space psychologists have another top tip for surviving long stretches in space: be creative. Writing or painting are good choices. As is making new 'friends' ...

Cosmonaut cockroach

Two Mir cosmonauts say they once discovered a stowaway cockroach that came up with a supply ship. To amuse themselves, they gave him a name, Grisha, and made him the honorary third member of the crew.

Making friends with a cockroach might sound like evidence of severe mental breakdown to most people. But Russian mind-doctors think not.

As well as general depression, fear, anxiety, loneliness and homesickness seem to be the most common astronaut problems. Apart from talking to people at home (and if you don't get on with your family, this might not be the best idea), how do you think you could cope?

1. Learn a relaxation technique to help with anxiety. You might try muscle relaxation. Pick a muscle and hold it tight for a few seconds. Then relax it. Do this to as many muscles as possible in turn.

2. Don't think all the time about your worries. Decide to spend only half an hour a day thinking about what's bothering you. The rest of the time, try to focus on what's happening around you.

3. Don't drink too much coffee — it can make you feel jittery.

These tips should help — at least in the short term. In the future, it's possible that psychologists will be able to come up with better ways to fight the problem. But then in the future everything could change. Chapter Ten will show you the way ...

THE FUTURE

Inflatable spacecraft, self-healing ship 'skin', luxury cruiseliners — destination: the Moon ... Not the ramblings of a sci-fi writer, but real projects with cash behind them.

In thirty or forty years, space planes could be taking off for the Moon as often as aeroplanes from London to New York. The trips won't be cheap. But they'll cost a lot less than the US$20 million paid by first ever space tourist Dennis Tito.

And while the tourists are having fun, hard-working astronauts will have a whole new world of kit to play with.

Inflate and escape

European engineers hope the International Space Station escape capsule of the future will look like a giant shuttlecock, with a vast blow-up heat shield. This inflatable shield will also act as a parachute to slow the craft as it descends. It is made from ceramic fibres – designed to withstand a blistering 1,000°C of heat during its return to Earth.

*But some tests of a recent experimental space shuttlecock scored only a **B−**.*

In July 2002, it launched from a Russian submarine, to disappear in a remote area of eastern Russia on its return. The lead engineer was dismayed: *'The whole area is populated by only 100 bears and a few soldiers, so it may take us days or weeks to find it!'*

Brilliant brainwaves

Space agencies will need plenty of brilliant brainwaves like the inflatable heat shield to help astronauts go where no one has gone before.

They're likely to use some of the following contenders for space's Award for Astonishing Potential.

See what you make of them.

CONTENDER NUMBER ONE: _ _ _ _ _ _ _ _ _ _ _ CARBON NANOTUBES

These very tiny, hollow tubes are made from a substance called carbon. By stacking the tubes together, scientists hope to build incredibly strong but lightweight materials – perfect for use in spacecraft.

If a carbon nanotube could give an interview, this is how it might go:

Bill Brain: *Good evening, folks. I have with me in the studio tonight our first contender: a carbon nanotube. Nanotube, can you tell us about your strengths?*

Nanotube: HA HA, THAT'S IT! I'M AS STRONG AS THEY GET BUT UNBELIEVABLY TINY! ABOUT SIX HUNDRED TIMES TOUGHER THAN STEEL!

Brain: *How tiny — exactly?*

Nanotube: SO SMALL THAT YOU CAN'T SEE ME!

Brain: *You're avoiding the question.*

Nanotube: WELL, A NANOMETRE IS ONE THOUSAND MILLIONTH OF A METRE ACROSS. I'M ONLY VERY SLIGHTLY LONGER THAN THAT.

Brain: *If you're so minute, how do you explain your incredible strength?*

Nanotube: IT'S ALL IN THE DESIGN! IMAGINE CHICKEN WIRE ROLLED INTO A CYLINDER — THAT'S ME. BUT UNLIKE CHICKEN WIRE, I'M VERY, VERY, VERY RIGID. NO FOXES WOULD GET PAST A CARBON NANOTUBE FENCE, THAT'S FOR SURE!

CONTENDER NUMBER TWO: — — — — — — — — — —
SELF-HEALING SKIN

One of the biggest dangers in space is debris — a chunk colliding with a craft could leave a hole that would need to be repaired by a spacewalking astronaut, or a robot. But what if the hole could repair itself? It might sound crazy, but scientists are working on making this a reality.

— —

Brain: And so to our next contender: self-healing skin. Here we have a top marksman about to shoot a hole right through it. That's right, folks, we're going to fire a bullet into a special material made from long chemical molecules called ionomers.

Ready . . .

. . . FIRE!!

Now, I'm rushing to the spot — looking for the hole. But what's this? It's gone! Remarkable! It's a self-healing sheet!

In the studio with me, I have space science star Professor Karl Kosmoski. Professor, tell us why we would need such a material in space?

KOSMOSKI: For spacecraft skin, of course! A big space rock colliding with the craft would make a hole. But a self-healing skin covering the craft would quickly close up the puncture — keeping the cabin airtight and the crew safe.

CONTENDER NUMBER THREE: — — — — — — — — —
BODY-PROTECTING BRICKS

The first astronauts to live on Mars will need protection from dangerous space radiation. They'll need homes and laboratories built from bricks that will keep them safe.

— —

Brain: And the final contender might look like a pile of bricks, but it represents a lot more than that. Imagine this, folks: you've spent six months in a craft on a journey to Mars. Danger all round. You arrive on the planet — and there are deadly new dangers. Over to you, Professor.

KOSMOSKI: Well, Mars has very little atmosphere and a very weak magnetic field. Why might this be dangerous?

Brain: I'm supposed to be asking the questions!

KOSMOSKI: I am asking this of myself! This means there is very little protection from cosmic rays. Astronauts and cosmonauts cannot lug special materials all the way from Earth to make shelters. No — they need to make them on the planet's surface. And they can! With a special recipe, they should be able to make bricks that will shield them from the rays!

Brain: Thank you, professor.

And for those of you who would like that recipe, here it is now.

1. Gather sand-like substance from Mars's surface
2. Mix it with a little bit of plastic powder brought from Earth.
3. Heat it.

The result: radiation-shielding bricks to use for building shelters.

Ready to pick your winner? It's a tough one. Perhaps first you should know about scientists' best bets for powering the craft of the future. Can you tell which of the following are real projects being worked on by scientists:

1. A craft powered by the light energy from the Sun?
2. An anti-gravity launching system?
3. A space plane propelled by cooking chocolate?
4. Magnetic levitation rails — a craft would fire along them and up into space?
5. Nuclear reactor rockets?

Answers:

1. Experimental craft designed to be powered by the Sun's energy have already been built. Ultra-thin, mirror-like 'solar sails' trap individual particles of light from the Sun. The energy from this moving light is transferred to the craft, pushing it along. Craft fitted with solar sails would travel slowly at first, but could eventually reach staggering speeds of up to 240,000 km/h.

2. Many scientists think an anti-gravity device is impossible. But researchers working for at least one highly respected company in England think there's a chance it might work. They're conducting secretive experiments on anti-gravity right now.

3. Sadly, no one's yet working on a chocolate-fuelled propulsion system.

4. NASA thinks magnetic levitation tracks might one day replace the launch pad, and its researchers are testing experimental tracks. 'Mag-lev' trains already exist. Rather than sliding along in contact with the track, they hover just above it — meaning they can travel much, much faster.

5. Engineers at NASA are developing ways of using nuclear power to send a craft into deep space. An on-board nuclear reactor could provide 100 times more power than today's rocket engines and keep a craft going for a lot longer. NASA thinks nuclear power could slash travel times. With existing technology, it would take at least six months to travel to Mars. With a nuclear engine, it could take just six weeks.

So now you know about the futuristic craft components and ways they might travel. But what will they look like?

At the Advanced Space Transportation Program, NASA experts predict the future of space travel.

Their concept vehicle for 2025 is the *Spaceliner 100*. Sleek and pointy-nosed, it looks a lot like a present-day supersonic plane. The Spaceliner 100 might launch using mag-lev tracks and pick up its passengers from an 'aero-spaceport'.

But NASA and the other major space agencies aren't the only organizations with a vision of the future. Many believe there is a lot of money to be made from space tourists. One Dutch architect has even come up with detailed plans for a far-out hotel.

TaKe a BReaK FROM EaRTH aND LiVe THE HiGH LiFe!

YOU'LL BE OVER THE MOON WITH OUR FABULOUS LUNAR LEISURE RESORT. WAKE UP IN YOUR VERY OWN HABITATION CAPSULE!

WALK UP ONE OF THE TWIN TALL TOWERS FOR BREAKFAST — AND FLY DOWN IN A SUIT WITH BAT-LIKE WINGS!

But don't run off to pack your bags just yet. It's very unlikely that this hotel will be up and running before at least 2050. Perhaps you shouldn't pin all your hopes on the Moon, either. Other space entrepreneurs have different plans:

1. One company says it will use 12 empty NASA fuel-tanks to build a ring-shaped, rotating space hotel. It hopes the resort could be in orbit round Earth within ten years.

2. Another very wealthy American corporation plans to build a space cruise ship a kilometre long. The ship will fly from a position in Earth's orbit to the Moon and back.

But how will a tourist get to the rotating space resort, or the cruise ship – or into space, full stop? NASA won't lend a space shuttle for the job and the Russian Space Agency might find it needs all its craft for trips to the ISS.

There is one answer. But first a warning ...
If you don't like lifts, hold your stomach.
Now ... imagine this ...

A base station on Earth, much like an airport today, with restaurants and shops. At its heart, a giant tower tens of kilometres tall. Above the tower, a cable just a few centimetres wide, stretching up 47,000 kilometres into space. Partway up the cable, a station with hotels and laboratories. The only way to get there is in a space elevator, shooting up through the tower, along the cable, taking you on the ride of your life!

A lift into space? One of the first people to come up with this seemingly bonkers idea was a Russian engineer called Yuri Artsutanov, in 1960. Famous science-fiction writer Arthur C. Clarke loved the notion and wrote a book involving a space elevator in 1979. Most scientists thought the idea crazy. But two separate NASA teams recently did their calculations and decided it's possible. Incredibly difficult to build — but possible.

There's no doubt, though, that if a space elevator is ever built, it won't happen for many years. In the meantime, clamouring space tourists will need something else. They'll need a company to win the X Prize ...

Open to all

The X Prize Creed: We believe that space flight should be open to all — not just an elite cadre of government employees or the ultra-rich.

The X Prize Foundation, based in America, is offering US$10 million to the first company to build a craft that can go into space and return in one piece, and do it time after time. So while you're preparing for your astronaut training, you could do worse than come up with a brilliant design!

Mission to Mars

You might also use your time to plan for the big one —
a trip to Mars.

In January 2004, US President George W. Bush announced
plans to send astronauts back to the Moon (by about 2020),
and then to the Red Planet. As part of these plans,
engineers have been asked to come up with a completely new
spacecraft, to replace the shuttle. NASA will also have to
work hard to better understand how to help a crew cope with
a journey to another planet.

But if you're going to be the first person ever to set foot on
Mars, there are a few things you should know ...

TRAINING FILE

MARS, A.K.A. THE RED PLANET

LOCATION: 79 million kilometres from Earth
TEMPERATURE: Average −63⁰C
LENGTH OF YEAR: 687 Earth days
LENGTH OF DAY: 24 hours, 37 minutes
GRAVITY: About one-third of Earth's
NUMBER OF MOONS: Two

Dwight Dirkswood, Space Log.
Earthdate: 12 July 2030

It's been a long, hard mission. Six months without the taste of a freshly baked doughnut. Enough to drive any man insane. Like that pink haze out there. Slowing our descent ... and I can see ... I can see ... canyons! Rocks! Clouds! The largest volcano in the solar system! More rocks! Stretching on forever. A rock that looks just like a burger!

The surface of Mars is not welcoming. It's freezing, dry, rocky and, as far as anyone can tell, lifeless. Not at all like Earth. At least, not like your neighbourhood. Unless you happen to live in the Haughton Impact Crater in the high Arctic, that is.

Mars on Earth

Some 23 million years ago, an asteroid slammed into the ground in northern Canada. The result: a crater 20 kilometres wide. It's flesh-numbingly cold, bone dry and scattered with broken debris. A little bit like ... the surface of Mars.

Every summer, enthusiastic scientists gather here and work with NASA teams to try out new Mars suits, drive around in Mars buggies and live in a mock-up of a Mars landing pod.

What do you think a Mars spacesuit will look like?

Even NASA isn't sure yet. But they do know it won't look much like the bulky EMU. Mars explorers will have to be able to move around easily to study the planet. They'll need a light, flexible, smart 'bio-suit' that can monitor their heart rate and other vital signs and help them leap and jump about the planet. And this suit will have to weigh less than 27 kilograms – a quarter of the weight of the EMU.

At the Haughton Impact Crater, NASA can 'road-test' new designs with a gang of willing helpers. These wannabe Mars explorers hope they'll be almost perfectly prepared for the real thing.

There's no doubt that a mission to Mars would be the toughest yet. Only the cream of the world's crop of top astronauts will even be considered for selection.

Over to you ...

To earn yourself a chance of being among them, you'll have to start training. Right now.

Put this book in your pocket: go for a swim.

Come home, do your science homework.

Make sure you've got every chance of making your dreams about travelling into space come true.